DAYS OF AWE AND WONDER

HOLY ADVENTURES IN ADVENT AND CHRISTMAS

Bruce G. Epperly

Parson's Porch Books

Days of Awe and Wonder

ISBN: Softcover 978-1-936912-82-7

Copyright © 2013 by Bruce G. Epperly

All rights reserved. No part of this book may be reproduced or transmitted in any form or by any means, electronic or mechanical, including photocopying, recording, or by any information storage and retrieval system, without permission in writing from the publisher.

To order additional copies of this book, contact:

Parson's Porch Books
1-423-475-7308
www.parsonsporch.com

Parsons Porch Books is an imprint of Parson's Porch & Company (PP&C) in Cleveland, Tennessee. PP&C is an innovative non-profit organization which raises money by publishing books of noted authors, representing all genres. All donations from contributors and profits from publishing are shared with the poor.

To the congregation of South Congregational Church,
United Church of Christ,
Centerville, Massachusetts
and my Grandsons Jack and Jamie
in Whose Lives God is Still Speaking and Beauty
Abounds

THE ADVENT ADVENTURE

VIRTUALLY EVERY PARENT, IN THE midst of a road trip, hears an impatient child's question, "Are we there yet?" To the child, the question is quite reasonable. She's tired of waiting and wants to arrive at the promised destination, right now!

This same impatience can apply to our adventures of faith. The desire to "get there" can be the lure that takes us from complacency to creativity and apathy to action. Advent is a time of holy impatience. During the Advent season, we wait for something we can't fully understand, a coming reality that is larger than we can imagine yet constantly calling us forward. We dream of a better day for ourselves and our loved ones. Although it is easy to succumb to the stark realism of a world characterized by conflict, consumerism, political gridlock, and planetary destruction, there is the deep down hope that we can change and that the world can change as well. We want to get there – to experience God's world of Shalom, the hoped-for Christmas spirit, and our higher selves right now! But, sometimes the distance between dream and reality overwhelms us.

Advent is a time in which we strive to be awake. We train our eyes for the slightest glimmer of

Christ's coming. We look for the emergence of a star on the horizon and the birth of something we cannot fully describe in our hearts and in the world. We live in a time of hope and anticipation: what we hope for is not yet here and we know that there is no guarantee that it will come. Still we dream of a holy adventure, and the possibility that a hovel houses a savior and a baby's cry ushers in an age of peace and planetary healing.

Long before the modern phenomenon of Black Friday and the post-Halloween Christmas sales, Advent was a time of spiritual examination, characterized by solemnity and fasting. Today, in the days prior to Christmas, we seldom fast and, in fact, must try our hardest to remain healthy and sober amid the flurry of obligatory holiday parties, even in congregational contexts.

Still, Advent is not all solemnity. A popular Christmas song of an earlier era proclaims, "We need a little Christmas, right this very moment." Although church musicians and preachers wrestle with whether or not to sing Christmas carols during Advent, without the dream of the Christ child and the coming of God's light, Advent would be a time of hopelessness. We would be waiting endlessly for nothing in particular like the characters from *Waiting for Godot*. With the characters of W.H. Auden's Christmas oratorio *For the*

Time Being, written in the darkest days of World War II, "we who must die demand a miracle."

Yes, if we are honest, deep down we demand a miracle, the emergence of something that will change everything. Advent spirituality asks us to contemplate our own complicity in the crises we face and our temptation to accept the world of violence, starvation, and conflict as the norm for human existence. The challenges are overwhelming and our powers seem so limited. But, because of Advent and Christmas, we can hope again. We can live in expectation that help is on the way. We can, with the prophet Isaiah, "arise for our light has come." (Isaiah 60:1)

Advent is a hard season, and not just in terms of bitter wintry winds. Without the birth of a child and the hope of a new world, we are condemned to live like the characters of Narnia, ruled by forces of darkness, and living in a world in which "it is always winter but never Christmas." Still, on the horizon a light is shining. There is hope for transformation, found in the saving power birthed in Bethlehem. What was alive in the first century may burst forth in our own time, enabling us to become the change that we seek. The holy child may be born in us! Emmanuel is on the horizon – for even on the darkest night, God is with us and we will find our way!

Advent is an adventurous time and it is a time for awe and wonder, because despite the apathy and hard-heartedness of the world, good news persists, and little children can still dream of star-filled nights and wandering magi, presents under a tree, family joy, and a little child leading us to salvation.

As you live the days of Advent, take time feel the contrast of now and not yet. Take time to look deeply at your tendencies to stand in the way of God's vision of peace and healing. Pause, amid the pre-Christmas rush, to gaze more deeply toward God's horizon of hope and your hope of the Christ Child being born in you. Let us begin our Advent Adventure with a prayer from Howard Thurman. Let this be our Advent affirmation and guide as we seek God's future on the pathway to Bethlehem:

> All around us worlds are dying and new worlds are being born; All around us life is dying and life is being born.
>
> The fruit ripens on the tree; the roots are silently at work in the darkness of the earth Against the time when there shall be new leaves, fresh blossoms, green fruit.
>
> Such is the growing edge!

It is the extra breath from the exhausted lung, the one more thing when all else has failed, the upward reach of life when weariness closes in upon all endeavor.

This is the basis of hope in moments of despair, the incentive to carry on when times are out of joint and persons have lost their reason; the source of confidence When worlds crash and dreams whiten into ash.

The birth of a child – life's most dramatic answer to death –

This is the growing edge incarnate.

Look well to the growing edge![1]

---

[1] Howard Thurman, *The Growing Edge* (Richmond, IN: Friends United Press, 1956), 180.

Advent reminds us that, regardless of how far we have fallen from grace, we are and can become children of the growing edge, lighting the way for Christ's coming in our time. Christ is coming: Look well to the growing edge!

+++

A Note about Your Daily Advent Adventures

Each day's meditation has four parts with the goal of moving from reflection to action and back again to prayer:

- A passage from scripture and a reflection on its meaning for people today
- An affirmative prayer to be repeated throughout the day
- A simple action intended to connect the scripture and reflection to the concreteness of your daily life
- A prayer that joins contemplation and action in healing the world

I encourage you to take as much time as you need but try to spend at least ten minutes daily on each day's meditation. If possible, begin with a few minutes of silence, and then read reflectively, meditate on the spiritual affirmation, and consider ways to embody the suggested action throughout the day. Close with prayer and a few moments of silence. In the course of the day, repeat the affirmation – you might write it on a note card – and look for opportunities to integrate the suggested activity with the events of the day. Your world will be transformed and you will experience God's presence in the pre-Christmas busyness, giving a glow to the lines at the department store and a sense of holiness to every Christmas greeting. May you experience God's blessings on your Advent adventures!

THE FIRST DAY OF ADVENT

LIVING IN HOPE OF GOD'S REALM OF SHALOM

God shall judge between the nations, and shall arbitrate for many peoples; they shall beat their swords into plowshares, and their spears into pruning hooks; nation shall not lift up sword against nation, neither shall they learn war any more. O House of Jacob, come let us walk in the light of God. (Isaiah 2:5)

Advent begins with a dream. An impossible dream of swords beaten into plowshares, spears into pruning hooks, and a world in which nations shall, as the gospel song proclaims, "Study war no more." Without a dream to guide us, we will eventually perish. Even when we turn away from God's vision for this good Earth, we feel the presence of the possibility of a different way of life, the vision of walking in God's light.

In a world of terrorist threats, cyber warfare, and drone attacks, the Advent dream of a peaceable realm seems far off. But, the holy adventures of the Spirit lead us onward even when the horizon appears to be receding. God's Spirit lures us forward with dreams of a better day.

Advent is the in-between time. The child of promise, the hope of Israel, lived among us, born in a stable, teaching and healing, welcoming nuisances and nobodies, and triumphing over death. Though Christmas is just over three weeks away, we hum the carols of "peace on earth, good will to all" and "silent night, holy night, all is calm, all is bright," despite the stories of violence on the front page and the evening news. Advent reminds us of the fierce urgency of now. We cannot be content with a world in which millions of children die of malnutrition, military expenses outstrip school budgets, and parents in Appalachia, Harlem, and Cape Cod see hope dimming in their children's eyes.

In an era of political polarization, let us as followers of Jesus agree on one thing, that every child deserves a safe place to live and healthy food to eat. One step is enough to create a movement that brings us together, despite our theological and political differences, to be God's companions in healing the Earth. Our Advent adventure calls us, and everyone else, to "walk in the light of God."

Affirmation: I am an instrument of God's peace.

Action: Today, consider what one thing you can do to be God's partner in beating swords into plowshares – in your household, community, congregation, and nation. How can you be God's messenger of peace in every encounter? How can my words and thoughts bring greater peace to the world?

Holy One, we thank you for a vision greater than our self-interest that lures us toward far horizons. Help us become instruments of your peace and companions in your peaceable realm so that every child is fed, laughter replaces tears, and unity overcomes alienation. In the name of the Prince of Peace. Amen.

+++

THE SECOND DAY OF ADVENT

ALIVE IN CHRIST

So you also must consider yourselves dead to sin and alive to God in Christ Jesus. (Romans 6:11)

It seems surprising to reflect on the resurrection during the Advent season. We identify resurrection with Holy Week and Easter and God's triumph over death in all its forms. Still, I suggest that we need to experience resurrection throughout the year. As a season of reflection, Advent hope is grounded not only in the incarnation of Jesus of Nazareth, and his birth among the most vulnerable and powerless persons of his time, and his message of God with us, but also in the daily struggle against physical, emotional, spiritual, and relational death.

During Advent, we seek courage to live by the affirmation that nothing can separate us from the love of God in Christ Jesus our Lord. (Romans 8:38-39) Many of us are our own worst enemies. Our own sense of guilt, failure, and shame separate us, in our own eyes, from God's love. The author of today's reading, the early Christian leader Paul, takes another approach to his past. He regrets his persecution of the early Christian movement. He knows he has blood on his hands and that he can never restore the lives of those who have died as a result of his passion to persecute the Jesus movement. Despite the legality of his acts, Paul will always remember his complicity in deaths of Jesus' followers. But, in light of resurrection hope, he is dead to sin and can let go of the burdens of the past and become a new creation in Christ Jesus.

Advent calls us to come alive. We can begin anew. We can become free of what stands between us and abundant life. We aren't there yet, as Paul notes in his Letter to the Philippians. But, the horizons of Advent inspire our spiritual adventures one day at a time. Resurrection beckons us forward, promising new life today and the hope of life everlasting in God's realm of Shalom.

Affirmation: I am alive in Christ. I am born anew every day.

Action: The Apostle Paul proclaims, "If anyone be in Christ, he is a new creation; if anyone be in Christ, she is a new creation." (2 Corinthians 5:17) Often our relationships with loved ones, fellow congregants, and co-workers are stuck in the past. We are governed by grudges, guilt, and unhealthy behaviors. Today, take a few minutes to reflect on the quality of your relationships. Is there anyone with whom you need to make a new start and explore new and healthy behaviors? If so, ask God to show you ways to participate in healing the relationship. Recognizing your own limits and the reality of others' responses, consider taking one small step toward becoming a new creation in relationship to a person in your life.

God of new beginnings, wake us up to wonder and beauty. Stir us to new life and healthy relationships. Help us claim your resurrection power so that we might live fully and freely as your companions in bringing justice, beauty, and reconciliation to this good Earth. In Christ's name. Amen.

+++

THE THIRD DAY OF ADVENT

WE LIVE IN A RAINBOW WORLD

"When the bow is in the clouds, I will see it and remember the everlasting covenant between God and every living creature of all flesh that is on the earth." God said to Noah, "This is the sign of the covenant that I have established between me and all flesh that is on the earth." (Genesis 9:16-17)

Ancient storytellers of the Middle East describe a great flood that brought chaos and destruction to the Earth. Eventually the flood waters subsided and human and non-human animals began to rebuild their lives. Our Hebraic parents saw God's hand in both the flood and the restoration of the Earth. While I do not personally believe that God destroys cities and species to punish the Earth for humanity's sins, I recognize that our actions have consequences and leave in their wake creation or destruction. They bring us nearer or draw us further from God's Advent vision of the peaceable realm.

Many people see the story of a great flood as merely a myth, irrelevant to twenty-first century people. While the events described in myths may not be factual, a living myth, such as the story of the great flood, points to deeper realities of life and charts the textures of our relationship with God. The Hebraic story of the great flood finds its meaning in divine faithfulness rather than human imperfection. God makes an everlasting covenant with all flesh. God proclaims God's care for osprey and whales, fireflies and foxes, geese and grasshoppers, Portuguese water dogs and people like us. God marks God's care by setting a multicolored rainbow in the heavens. Every time the people look at the rainbow, they are to remember God's love for them and all creation.

We can explain a rainbow in naturalistic terms, caused by light reflecting through water droplets. We can also affirm a deeper and more holy naturalism in which everyday events reflect and point us toward divine wisdom. Today, the multicolored arc reminds us that God loves diversity. Just look at your family, no two members are alike. Look at your garden, the woodlands and beaches, and the amazing diversity of flora and fauna. The diversity of human and non-human life is an invitation to awe, wonder, and affirmation. Advent awakens us to the many ways to celebrate life, the diverse pathways of race, spirituality, ethnicity, and sexuality. Diversity is not a fall from grace but a reflection of divine love and creativity.

Although Advent is not typically associated with rainbows, Advent invites us to awaken to the faithfulness of God in this rainbow world. Rejoice in the wonder of each face and hue, and the gifts of many species and nations.

Affirmation: I give thanks for the diversity of God's world.

Action: Take time to look for diversity in your neighborhood. Notice the varieties of flora and fauna and human cultures and ethnicities. Look deeply for beauty in diversity and, if the occasion arises, reach out to someone from another race, community, or culture.

Artist of Adventure, awaken us to the beauty of diversity. Inspire us to celebrate all the colors of the rainbow. Create in us spacious hearts, large enough

> *to affirm our own community and delight in the uniqueness of other lands and cultures. In Jesus' name. Amen.*

+++

THE FOURTH DAY OF ADVENT

CHRIST COMES TO US IN EVERY MOMENT

> *From the fig tree learn its lesson: as soon as its branch becomes tender and puts forth its leaves, you know that summer is near. So also, when you see all these things, you know that he is near, at the very gates. Truly I tell you, this generation will not pass away until all these things have taken place. Heaven and earth will pass away, but my words will not pass away.* (Matthew 24:32-35)

Many people live in expectation of the end of the world as we know it. December 2012 brought hope and anxiety in those who anticipated a seismic shift in planetary life as a result of their interpretation of the Mayan calendar. Nearly every year, someone recalculates the prophetic numerology of the Bible and states without a doubt that Jesus will be coming in the near future, bringing both destruction and new creation. For two thousand years, the anticipated end of the world and with it the literal Second Coming of Jesus has come and gone, leaving both scorn and disappointment in its wake.

Advent speaks of the return of Christ. The return may not be as dramatic as Biblical doomsayers predict. In fact, if we listen to Jesus' words from Matthew 24, Jesus may be coming to you this very moment and you need to be awake to hear his voice amid the many demands of daily life.

A bumper sticker announces, "Jesus is coming. Look busy!" Busyness is not the issue; the issue is awareness. Will we be awake to the "signs of the times" in our daily lives and the world round us? Will we carefully observe the growth of the fig tree, acting appropriately and faithfully in our current situation?

Salvation is not a one-time affair. Every moment can be decisive in our relationship to God and our neighbors. As Paul says in 2 Corinthians 6:2:

For God says, "At an acceptable time I have listened to you, and on a day of salvation I have helped you." See, now is the acceptable time; see, now is the day of salvation!

God invites us to freedom and joy right now. God invites us to see Jesus' coming in the face of a young child in need of school supplies, a parent struggling with substance abuse, the familiar face across the breakfast table, and in the economic and environmental crises of our time. Healing can't wait. Jesus stands at the door and knocks. If you open the door and let him into your heart, your life will be transformed and every day will be a holy adventure.

Affirmation: I open to God's presence in every encounter.

Action: Stay awake and be alert to "God-moments" and "Christ comings." Listen for God's voice in the morning news and in encounters with your companions. Hear God's call at the checkout stand. Throughout the day, ask God to awaken you to opportunities to bring healing to the world.

Holy One, remind us that Christ is with us now and that we don't have to wait for heaven to experience everlasting life. Awaken us to your salvation and inspire us to bring your healing to the least of these in our midst. In Christ's name. Amen.

of the world and with it the literal Second Coming of Jesus has come and gone, leaving both scorn and disappointment in its wake.

Advent speaks of the return of Christ. The return may not be as dramatic as Biblical doomsayers predict. In fact, if we listen to Jesus' words from Matthew 24, Jesus may be coming to you this very moment and you need to be awake to hear his voice amid the many demands of daily life.

A bumper sticker announces, "Jesus is coming. Look busy!" Busyness is not the issue; the issue is awareness. Will we be awake to the "signs of the times" in our daily lives and the world round us? Will we carefully observe the growth of the fig tree, acting appropriately and faithfully in our current situation?

Salvation is not a one-time affair. Every moment can be decisive in our relationship to God and our neighbors. As Paul says in 2 Corinthians 6:2:

> *For God says, "At an acceptable time I have listened to you, and on a day of salvation I have helped you." See, now is the acceptable time; see, now is the day of salvation!*

God invites us to freedom and joy right now. God invites us to see Jesus' coming in the face of a young child in need of school supplies, a parent struggling with substance abuse, the familiar face across the breakfast table, and in the economic and environmental crises of our time. Healing can't wait. Jesus stands at the door and knocks. If you open the door and let him into your heart, your life will be transformed and every day will be a holy adventure.

Affirmation: I open to God's presence in every encounter.

Action: Stay awake and be alert to "God-moments" and "Christ comings." Listen for God's voice in the morning news and in encounters with your companions. Hear God's call at the checkout stand. Throughout the day, ask God to awaken you to opportunities to bring healing to the world.

Holy One, remind us that Christ is with us now and that we don't have to wait for heaven to experience everlasting life. Awaken us to your salvation and inspire us to bring your healing to the least of these in our midst. In Christ's name. Amen.

THE FIFTH DAY OF ADVENT

PRAY WITHOUT CEASING

All the followers of Jesus were constantly devoting themselves to prayer, together with certain women, including Mary, the mother of Jesus, as well as his brothers. (Acts 2:14)

Following the Ascension, the followers of Jesus searched for guidance as they continued the Savior's ministry. They needed new leadership and wisdom in sharing good news to all humankind. Rather than trusting their own efforts alone, they sought God's guidance for the adventures ahead. They devoted themselves to prayer. We don't know the prayer forms employed by the early church. We can imagine that their prayers included gratitude, adoration, intercession, and petition. Perhaps they were motivated by Jesus' counsel to "ask, seek, and knock," trusting that in the process of calling to God, God would reach out to them, giving them as the apostle Paul proclaims, "more than we can ask or imagine." (Ephesians 3:20)

We need guidance to face the individual, congregational, national, and planetary challenges of our time. There are no easy answers or solutions to issues of congregational growth, personal decision-making, economics and politics, and planetary survival. We need to pray for divine guidance, insight, and empowerment. Prayer connects us with a deeper wisdom and gives us energy to fulfill our personal and corporate vocations. Even if you worry about your ability to pray, you can "ask, seek, and knock," and although the answers may not always be clear, you will receive guidance enough for one step at a time.

Affirmation: I pray without ceasing. Surprises and interruptions call me to prayer.

Action: Experiment with praying boldly. Your prayers don't need to be sophisticated or even articulate. Author Ann Lamott asserts that prayer has three essential elements, "help, thanks, and wow." Simply take time to pray throughout the day, asking God for wisdom, guidance, courage, patience, and fortitude. Give thanks for the wonder of life and rejoice in life's beauty.

Holy One, you have promised that you will give us more than we can ask or imagine if we simply ask.

Help us to bold in our prayers and open to the wisdom you give us. Help us to not only expect miracles, acts of power in our lives, but also accept miracles when they come our way. When we receive guidance, give us the courage to act as your companions in healing the world. In Jesus' name. Amen.

+++

THE SIXTH DAY OF ADVENT

THE WORLD IS CHARGED WITH GOD'S GRANDEUR

Blessed be the Lord, the God of Israel, who alone does marvelous things. Blessed by God's glorious name forever; may God's glory fill the whole earth. Amen and amen. (Psalm 72:18-19)

In describing his mystical encounter with God in the Jerusalem Temple, Isaiah proclaims that the whole earth is filled with God's glory. Advent invites us to awaken to glory. Rabbi Abraham Joshua Heschel proclaims that radical amazement is at the heart of religious experience. In that same spirit, Louis Armstrong sings, "I say to myself it's a wonderful world."

As we ponder, Jesus' birth, we can imagine the wonder that Mary felt as her child grew within her. This same wonder accompanies the growth of every child from conception to birth and then beyond. At such moments, mothers and fathers can experience the utter amazement of new life emerging from the smallest of beginnings.

Each morning God does marvelous things. As poet Gerard Manley Hopkins exclaims,

> The world is charged with the grandeur of God. It will flame out, like shining from shook foil; It gathers to a greatness like the ooze of oil.

Each morning Christ is born anew within us and we can choose to Christ-bearers, rejoicing in God's wonderful world and adding to the beauty of life. Glory guides the path of all who open to the amazing grace of God's wonderful world.

Affirmation: I rejoice in God's wonderful world.

Action: If you are able, listen to a version of Louis Armstrong's "It's a Wonderful

World." [2] Throughout the day, open to wonder, the pure amazement of being alive. Look at the faces of children, spouses, friends, and passersby, along with scudding clouds, the rising moon, and the animals in your home and neighborhood. Rejoice in their intricate beauty and treat all creation with love and respect.

Holy God, wake us up to beauty; inspire us to wonder; lure us toward amazement that each day's journey might be an adventure of the spirit and each night's rest an opportunity to trust your care for all creation. In Jesus' blessed name. Amen.

+++

THE SEVENTH DAY OF ADVENT

GOD IS FAITHFUL IN LIFE AND DEATH

The grass withers, the flower fades; but the word of God will stand forever. (Isaiah 40:8)

---

[2] http://www.youtube.com/watch?v=0lJEYWOdjUo

As a pastor, I live with the ever-present reality of death. In the course of my first two months at South Congregational Church, three members passed away. Our congregation lost three good friends. Regardless of our medical advancements, the mortality rate remains 100% and many of us will die too soon as a result of accidents, suicide, and incurable illness.

"In the midst of life, we are surrounded by death," the Reformer Martin Luther proclaimed. The reality of death can rob life of meaning and fill us with fear; it can also invite us to "count our days that we might gain a wise heart." (Psalm 90:12) Martin Luther also affirmed that "in the midst of death, we are surrounded by life." God is trustworthy and God's word and wisdom, God's energy of love and transformation endure forever. Our trust in life and death is in the One, who has loved us into life, guided us with every new day, and will receive us with loving arms at the moment of death. The scriptural affirmation, "Nothing can separate us from the love of God in Christ Jesus our Lord," invites us to live fully and courageously, embracing each moment as holy and unrepeatable. Remember that you are in God's hands in all the changes of life and that every moment can be an opportunity for praise and compassion.

Affirmation: I trust God in life and death. Nothing can separate me from the love of God.

Action: A wise teacher reminds us that the greatest gift is to be born into loving arms and die surrounded by loving arms. Knowing that you are the hands and arms of Christ, prayerfully reflect on how you can participate in the care of our community's most vulnerable children and adults. This act of compassion may involve a financial gift, phone call, visit to a local care facility, or offering to give a family member respite care. Ask God to guide your hands and feet in ways that embody simple kindness to vulnerable persons.

God of life and death, we place our whole lives in your care. Help us to trust our lives and deaths to you so that we have the courage and compassion to reach out to the most vulnerable in our midst and so that we might, at the end of our days, have confidence that your love is eternal. In the name of the Risen Christ. Amen.

+++

Bruce G. Epperly

THE EIGHTH DAY OF ADVENT

LIVING IN HARMONY WITH ALL GOD'S CHILDREN

> *May the God of steadfastness and encouragement grant you to live in harmony with one another, in accordance with Christ Jesus, so that together you may with one voice glorify the God and Father of our Lord Jesus Christ. Welcome one another, therefore, just as Christ has welcomed you, for the glory of God.* (Roman s 15:5-7)

A Navajo blessing proclaims, "With beauty all around me, I walk." The Christian life is intended to beautiful. Our lives are our gifts to God and our calling is to give God a beautiful world in which diversity and contrast contribute to the well-being of all. In today's reading, the apostle Paul is speaking to both Jews and Gentiles. He imagines the church as a dynamic body, made up of diverse and interdependent cells and organs. The health of the whole depends on the well-being of each part, and the whole supports the well-being of each part. Diversity leads to beauty, and not division. Harmony is the gift of creative diversity and this means that a healthy congregation, like a healthy body, is enriched when every part realizes its vocation and has a voice in the melody of faith. Today's reading invites us to be persons of stature, able to embrace contrasting feelings and welcome diversity without losing our own growing spiritual center.

Welcome diversity today, whether it is ethnic, political, racial, sexual, or theological. When we go beyond polarization and open to God's intricate artistry, we discover a world in which every face reminds of us Jesus and different viewpoints call us to friendship and love.

Affirmation: With beauty all around me, I walk. I live in harmony with all creation.

Action: Intentionally reach out to someone from a diverse ethnic group or political or theological persuasion. Without making a fuss, listen to their unique perspectives and experiences, and if the occasion arises, share your unique experiences and viewpoints in a welcoming and respectful way.

Artist of wonder and beauty, we thank you for a world of diversity: a world of whales sporting off Nantucket; osprey nesting on Cape Cod; polar bears in the Arctic; and humankind in all its wondrous diversity. Remind us that beauty requires contrast and otherness. Help us to share in your quest for beauty in every aspect of our lives and in all the flora and fauna of this good Earth. In Christ's name. Amen.

+++

THE NINTH DAY ADVENT

LIVING HOPEFULLY

But we do not want you to be uninformed, brothers and sisters, about those who have died, so that you may not grieve as others do who have no hope. For since we believe that Jesus died and rose again, even so, through Jesus, God will bring with him those who have died. (I Thessalonians 4:13-14)

One of my callings as a pastor is to visit the recently bereaved and officiate at the funerals and memorial services of loved ones. Death punctuates life. Those we love are no longer here. Even though they may have been taken away from us years long before their physical deaths as a result of strokes, dementia, and Alzheimer's, the pain of separation may remain intense and often unendurable. Like the phenomenon of the phantom limb syndrome, our thoughts and emotions reach out to them, but there is no longer anything to which to reach toward. The apostle Paul was acquainted with grief. He had likely outlived his parents and experienced the deaths of many members of the Christian movement as a result of Roman persecution. He felt the pain of separation from loved ones.

Our emotional pain is real and should never be denied, when a beloved person is taken away from us as the result of accident, aging, illness, or suicide. Paul encourages us to grieve. He knows that healing will not come without embracing the necessary and unexpected losses of life. An open heart feels both pain and joy. Denial of our losses deadens the spirit and emotions, and stands in the way of God's healing touch. Grieve hopefully, the apostle Paul counsels, because although those we love are separated from us for a time, they are in God's loving care and we will be reunited with them in God's everlasting realm of love.

When I introduce myself as a pastor, I never know what the response will be. Sometimes, people quickly end the conversation, worrying that I may try to convert them; other times they apologize for having just said a word that they believe offends me; still other times, folks ask questions of life and death. Recently, after asking what I did for a living, a new companion at a local coffee house asked: "My cousin just committed suicide. Where is he now?" While the afterlife is a mystery, despite best-selling books on near death experiences, I surprised her by saying, "I believe she is God's hands." She expected me to invoke divine judgment and hell-fire and brimstone for what some call the unpardonable sin. But, neither Paul nor I believe that death ends our relationship with God. Love is stronger than death. As of my mentors, Ernie Campbell, preaching professor and pastor of Riverside Church in Manhattan noted, "There are only two kinds of people in the world: those who are in God's hands and know it, and those who are in God's hands and don't."

Paul's confidence in the resurrection inspires him to embrace grief knowing that nothing can separate us from the love of God in Christ Jesus our Lord. The present may be uncertain, Paul recognizes, but the victory has been won, our future is God's hands, and God's Advent brings hope of everlasting love and life. We can grieve, expressing the whole range of emotions because we are in God's hands forevermore.

Affirmation: My loved ones and I are in God's hands forever.

Action: Take time to reflect on persons who are grieving in your circle of friends and acquaintances. Surround them in prayer and if it is appropriate, reach out to them by making a phone call, inviting them to lunch, or taking a walk or coffee break.

Loving God, help us to embrace the grief of the world and our own grief, knowing that we are in your loving hands and that in life and death, we belong to God, and God will not lose any of God's beloved children. In Christ's Name. Amen.

+++

THE TENTH DAY OF ADVENT

I PROCLAIM CHRIST'S GOOD NEWS

For I will not venture to speak of anything except what Christ has accomplished through me to win obedience from the Gentiles, by word and deed, by the power of signs and wonders, by the power of the Spirit of God, so that from Jerusalem and as far around as Illyricum I have fully proclaimed the good news of Christ. Thus I make it my ambition to proclaim the good news. (Romans 15:18-20a)

The God described by the Hebraic and early Christian tradition constantly moves through the events of our lives and the world. Intimately connected with all things, God's presence and vision can be discerned in the flight of an osprey, the stars in the heavens, the moon over the ocean or desert, the babblings of a young child, and the wise words and actions of spiritual teachers from all continents.

In his words to the Romans, Paul acknowledges that his ministry is dependent of God's words and wisdom. His witness is a response to God's inspiration. Paul recognizes his own freedom and responsibility. He also affirms that he "can do all things through Christ who strengthens me." (Philippians 4:13) Christ is constantly providing us with insights and the energy to achieve them. When we open the door to Christ through prayer, meditation, service, recognizing God's wisdom in our deepest thoughts and emotions and in the faces of our loved ones and the least of these, great things happen. Radically aware of God's presence in his life, Paul makes a commitment to give God glory by constantly speaking the good news of Jesus Christ.

There are many ways to share good news: words and actions can heal. Our daily lives lived out in otherwise ordinary affairs can testify to God's love. We can, as Frederick Buechner says, listen to our lives, and then, in the words of Parker Palmer, let our lives speak as witnesses to good news wherever we go.

Affirmation: God is constantly speaking in my life and when I listen, I can by God's grace bring good news wherever I go.

Action: Quietly and prayerfully share your desire to hear God's inspiration in your life. Throughout the day, ask God to keep your senses open to God-moments emerging in everyday situations.

Loving God, the whole earth witnesses to your wisdom and love. Sometimes, however, I am forgetful that you also speak in my daily life, in insights, dreams, and encounters. Wake me up to your guidance and give me the courage to follow the path of Jesus each day of my life. In Christ's name. Amen.

+++

THE ELEVENTH DAY OF ADVENT

TRUSTING GOD'S PROMISES

> *After these things the word of the* LORD *came to Abram in a vision, "Do not be afraid, Abram, I am your shield; your reward shall be very great."…. He brought him outside and said, "Look toward heaven and count the stars, if you are able to count them." Then he said to him, "So shall your descendants be." And he believed the* LORD; *and the* LORD *reckoned it to him as righteousness.* (Genesis 15:1, 5-6)

Whenever God or one of God's messengers visits people, they often begin the encounter with the counsel, "Do not be afraid!" God knows – and we know – that there's much about which to be afraid. Psychiatrist Robert Jay Lifton notes that one of the most compelling images of survival after death is "biological immortality," the desire to have children and continue our family's lineage. Both Abram (Abraham) and his wife Sarah (Sarai) were afraid: they had been promised a sky full of descendants, but still they were childless. They feared that with their deaths, their family heritage would expire as well!

We are often afraid. Advent's future orientation invites us to reflect on those aspects of the future that are most frightening to us. For some of us, our fears are personal and constellate around questions such as: Will we have a happy old age or succumb to an incurable disease or lose our mental faculties through Alzheimer's? Will we have enough financial resources for retirement? Will we die alone, having outlived our family and closest friends, or be surrounded by loved ones? For others, relationships are a source of fear. We spend sleepless nights pondering: What will happen to our son or brother with disabilities when we die? Can we recover the spark of love that burned brightly once upon a time? Will I ever meet another life partner or will I live alone the rest of my life? Many of us also have global and national fears: Will we be able to respond to the threat of global warming? Can our nation recover economically? Will the next generation have as good a life as we had?

God responds to Abram's fears by inviting him to look at the heavens. God wanted Abram to see his life in a larger perspective, not just about one generation but as part of a vast cosmic journey which includes our human adventures.

During Advent, we are also challenged to see our lives from a bigger perspective than the present moment. We are invited to see our lives in light of God's vision for humankind and the planet. Our lives are part of a larger story – a communion of saints – that inspires and empowers. Our lives contribute to God's grand vision of humankind and planet Earth. What we do matters even if we live unnoticed. We can trust that our times are in God's hands and that, like an artist, God will weave our lives into a complex and adventurous tapestry.

Affirmation: I see my life as part of a larger human and planetary narrative in which my life makes a difference.

Action: Recognizing your connection with past and future, give thanks for the past that has made your life possible and ask for guidance as your actions shape the future. Live in the spirit of former United Nations Secretary General Dag Hammarskjold, who wrote:
> For all that has been – thanks!
> For all that shall be – yes!

God, whose love has been our hope in ages past and will be our hope in years to come, deliver us from fear of the future so that we might live joyfully and courageously in this Holy Now. Help us to greet the future with a big "yes," knowing that you have a vision for our lives and that when we follow your vision we bring abundance to ourselves and to this good Earth. In Christ's name. Amen.

+++

THE TWELFTH DAY OF ADVENT

WE ARE CONNECTED

But Ruth said, "Do not press me to leave you or to turn back from following you! Where you go, I will go; where you lodge, I will lodge; your people shall be my people, and your God my God. Where you die, I will die— there will I be buried. May the LORD *do thus and so to me, and more as well, if even death parts me from you!" When Naomi saw that she was determined to go with her, she said no more to her.* (Ruth 1:16-18)

The relationship between Ruth and Naomi is a model of "holy otherness." As the story goes, Naomi, her husband, and two sons leave Bethlehem and settle in Moab. Immigrants, seeking to make a new life in Moab during a time of famine in their own land, Naomi's sons meet and marry two Moabite women. Tragically, both sons and their father die, leaving three widows to fend for themselves. Orpah, Ruth's sister-in-law chooses to return to her Moabite family. Ruth chooses to remain with her mother-in-law, crossing the border to Israel, and entering an unfamiliar land. Ruth's future as an immigrant does not deter her. Her love for Naomi inspires her to face the uncertainties of being a stranger in a strange land. For Ruth, love is stronger than race or ethnicity. Her love for her mother-in-law enables her to claim every place as home. Ruth and Boaz, a wealthy farmer, fall in love, marry, and give birth to a generation of children leading to the birth of the great King David and, according to Biblical lore, to our Savior and Healer Jesus.

Advent's Shalom-vision awakens us to our common humanity. There is no "other." We are connected to one another, regardless of age, ethnicity, gender, economics, and sexuality. Our well-being is connected with the well-being of others, including people across the global whom we will never meet. Advent invites us to a rainbow-colored word in which we experience the "holy otherness" of people from other cultures, races, and nations. Open to God's creative diversity, we grow in spiritual stature and claim our vocation as companions in living out God's realm "on earth as it is in heaven."

Affirmation: I open to God's presence in persons from different cultures, races, ages, sexualities, and ethnicities.

Action: Regardless of your political persuasion or view about how we can best respond to issues of immigration, look for ways to welcome visitors and immigrants to our land. Be especially concerned with the impact of immigration laws on family unity. For example, consider the problems faced by children of immigrants, undocumented or illegal, who are separated from their parents when their parents are deported from the USA. How can we creatively support these children and their parents, regardless of how they got to our country? How can we help them, like our own children or grandchildren, live their dreams?

Holy God, we remember Ruth who traveled to a distant land, inspired by love for Naomi. We also remember the flight of Mary, Joseph, and Jesus to Egypt and their life as aliens in an unfamiliar land. Help us to seek the well-being of the immigrants in our midst, responding to their needs and welcoming them as Christ's children. In Jesus' name. Amen.

+++

Bruce G. Epperly

THE THIRTEENTH DAY OF ADVENT

LIVING LIVES OF PATIENCE AND HOLINESS

> *What sort of people ought you to be in leading lives of holiness and godliness, waiting for and hastening the coming of the day of God….But, in accordance with his promise, we wait for new heavens and a new earth, where righteousness is at home. Therefore, beloved, while you are waiting for these things, strive to be found by him at peace, without spot or blemish.* (I Peter 3:11b-12a, 14-15)

The first Christians lived in expectation of the Second Coming of Jesus and the creation of a "new heaven and new earth, where righteousness is at home." (I Peter 3:13) While they were chronologically mistaken about the time table of Jesus' return, there is wisdom in many of their "apocalyptic" (writings revealing the end of the old era and the beginning of Christ's reign on earth) reflections. Many of Jesus' followers, motivated by the shortness of time, believed that we needed to seize the moment and become citizens of God's realm in preparation for Jesus' literal return. Today, we need to become "kingdom people," living already as if God's vision is being embodied in the world. This means living in contrast to the ways of the world – greed, violence, materialism, alienation, consumerism, manipulation, infidelity – and walking in the path of Christ. This is especially difficult when consumerism crowds out Christ at Christmas! As the Apostle Paul proclaims, "Do not be conformed to this world, but be transformed by the renewing of your minds, so that you may discern what the will of God— what is is good and acceptable and perfect." (Romans 12:2)

The author of I Peter advises us to live at peace with God, without spot and blemish, while we await Christ's return. Although few of us today wait for a literal Second Coming or affirm the need for an earth-destroying cataclysm as a prelude to Christ's reign, we live with our own "apocalyptic" concerns – economic insecurity, the possibility of global climate change, the shift in global political and military power. The "end" may not be near, but still we recognize that the survival of the planet and the well-being of millions of starving and impoverished people require a new set of values, personally and corporately. Like our first century parents in the faith, we need to be guided by love, reconciliation, and care for the vulnerable; we need to be faithful and supportive in our relationships.

Today's reading asks us to examine our lives: What changes do we need to make to become self-aware citizens of God's realm of Shalom? Where do we need to seize the moment, living in relationship with Christ and open to God's new creation? How can we live as if Christ is beside us at this very moment?

Affirmation: I seek to be faithful to God in all my relationships. I cherish each moment as an opportunity to follow God's pathway of salvation and share God's love with others.

Action: Take time to experience watching the news or reading the newspaper as a call to prayer. What values are seen as important to a "good life" on commercials and television programs? Are these the values you want to embody as a follower of Jesus? Where does the local, national, and international news call you to make changes in your life or look at life differently? What can you do as one person to begin to live as if God's realm of Shalom is real and happening right now?

Holy One, who calls us to live by a vision of love, reconciliation, and justice, open our eyes to your presence in today's news. Open our hearts to the pain and the joy of life. Open our minds to new possibilities for personal and community transformation. Open our hands to reach out in service to Jesus our Savior. In Christ's name. Amen.

THE FOURTEENTH DAY OF ADVENT

LISTENING FOR GOD'S VOICE

Now God came and stood there, calling as before, "Samuel, Samuel." And Samuel said, "Speak for your servant is listening." (I Samuel 3:10)

In a time of national uncertainty, Samuel discovers that God is still speaking. According to the biblical narrative, the voice of God had become rare among the children of Israel. Even in the Temple, the priests were pursuing the desires of their own hearts and not attending to the voice of the One who had brought them forth from captivity to freedom and given them a land of promise. Still, as young Samuel began his internship with the Eli, the Temple priest, "the lamp of God had not yet gone out." (I Samuel 3:3)

Samuel hears a voice in the night, calling "Samuel, Samuel." At first, he assumes that his mentor Eli is calling for him. After the third call, Eli intuits that the voice comes from God and advises Samuel to ask the voice to speak directly to him. Although Samuel is just a young man, he receives a revelation and discovers his life's vocation.

As a practical theologian and pastor, I look for

the concrete applications of otherwise abstract theological doctrines. Many people assert, appropriately, that God is omnipresent. Ironically, they also assume that God is present everywhere except in their own lives or vocational quests. Sometimes, when they confess that the notion that God is constantly giving them wisdom and moving in their lives seems absurd – after all, they are mere mortals and frankly don't think God would condescend to speaking to them – I respond humorously, "What is it about God's presence in *all* things don't you understand? Do think God is everywhere except in your life? What's so special about you that you're the one person in the universe that God is not inspiring?"

As you listen to your life experiences, could it be that God is calling you in the events of your life and in your hunches and intuitions? Could a particular nudge or inspiration reflect God's guidance? Although it is always important to test our experiences with the wisdom of scripture, spiritual friends, and basic common sense, we need to be open to divine insight whenever it appears. We might even choose to follow Samuel prayerfully saying, "Speak, God, I am listening." Or, we might ask God for wisdom or insight into a particular situation. God is always speaking to us. Let us take time to listen for God's word and wisdom moving in our lives.

Affirmation: God is constantly inspiring me. I listen to God's wisdom in my life.

Action: Take time to open to God's presence prayerfully. If you are in need of insight or wisdom, or need direction in your life, ask God to respond to your deepest needs. Ask God if there is some person for whom you might be an answer to prayer or who would be benefitted by your outreach.

Holy One, we are grateful that you are still speaking in our lives. Help us to listen for your voice and respond in ways that bring joy to us and to others. In Christ's name. Amen.

+++

THE FIFTEENTH DAY OF ADVENT

SIGNS OF THE CHRIST

When John heard in prison what the Messiah was doing, he sent word by his disciples and said to him, "Are you the one who is to come, or are we to wait for

> *another?" Jesus answered them, "Go and tell John what you hear and see: the blind receive their sight, the lame walk, the lepers are cleansed, the deaf hear, the dead are raised, and the poor have good news brought to them. And blessed is anyone who takes no offence at me."* (Matthew 11:2-6)

What are the signs of Christ's coming? When some Christians consider the goal of history, they identify the Second Coming of Jesus with earthquake, fire, tsunami, and mass destruction. They assume that the true Christians will be "raptured" or raised up into the air to meet Jesus as he descends from the clouds, while non-believers are destroyed by hell-fire and brimstone. Such thinking has inspired the bumper sticker, "In case of rapture, this car will be driverless." Imagine the scene: cars careening down the roadways running down pedestrians who are unfortunate enough not to be among God's chosen ones.

Such violent and dualistic thinking is a far cry from Jesus' response to John. Recall that Jesus once proclaimed "I have come that they might have life, and have it abundantly." (John 10:10) The Messiah, God's Chosen One, comes – according to Jesus – to heal, liberate, and inspire hope. In Jesus of Nazareth, God comes bearing good news for all humankind. Jesus calls us to repent, turn around, and change our ways. Our repentance is the prelude to the healing of persons and communities.

Following Jesus today means sharing God's good news in thought, word, and deed. What might it mean for you to bring good news to the world? Where are you invited to bring good news that Christ is alive and people can have new life?

Affirmation: I share God's good news wherever I go.

Action: The Quakers have a saying, "Let your life speak." Our lives are our witness to our faith in Jesus and God's good news in the world. Prayerfully consider how you can be a bringer of "good news" today. Let your prayers take words and hands as you reach out to someone in need of experiencing God's good news.

Loving God, help us to be good news people. Help us to experience God's good news and share this good news with everyone we meet. In Jesus' name. Amen.

Bruce G. Epperly

THE SIXTEENTH DAY OF ADVENT

HEALING POWER

> *Now many signs and wonders were done among the people through the apostles....they even carried out the sick into the streets, and laid them on cots and mats, in order that Peter's shadow might fall on some of them as he came by. A great number of people would also gather from the towns around Jerusalem, bringing the sick and those tormented by unclean spirits, and they were all cured.* (Acts 5:12, 15-16)

We often expect too little from ourselves and too little from God. The early Christian movement lived in expectation that God would show up and miracles would happen. While we can't fully understand the nature of these first century acts of divine power, we are discovering the significance of mind-body-spirit medicine. Our thoughts and prayers can shape our overall health. Meditation not only connects us with God, but also promotes stress reduction, immune system functioning, and healthy blood pressure.

Jesus asserted that a person's faith can bring wholeness to their lives. While I believe that the miraculous events of scripture and Christian history are not "supernatural" and contrary to the laws of nature, I believe that we can experience quantum leaps of energy that transform cells and souls. I affirm that faith can contribute to our well-being. We live in a wonderful universe in which God's energy of love can burst forth at any moment. Our cells and souls are connected such a way that faith can be a tipping point.

In the last few decades, scientists have been studying the power of prayer and have discovered that our prayers for others can influence others' health. This has led physician Larry Dossey to proclaim that "prayer is good medicine." In an interdependent universe, our prayers can create a positive field of force around those for whom we pray, not only opening the door to a greater influx of divine energy but also shaping of environment in positive ways.

Today, we are learning that faith and medicine complement one another. We can, as physician Dale Matthews asserts, join "prayer and Prozac." We can integrate meditation and medication for our well-being and the well-being of others. The interplay of faith and medicine as reflections of God's aim at wholeness challenges us to take prayer seriously and to make our churches laboratories of prayer and healing touch. We may discover that wherever healing is present, whether through medicine or spiritual practices, God is its source. As we lift our hearts in prayer, let us expect great things from God and great things from ourselves as God's partners in healing the world.

Affirmation: My faith opens me to God's healing power.

Action: Prayer changes things. While they may not be omnipotent, our prayers can shape our lives and the lives of others. Make a commitment today to pray for your needs and the needs of others. Pray for planetary, social, and political issues.

Holy God, I open to your healing touch in my life. I lift up my prayers for those in need, for the sick and dying, and the oppressed. Help me to expect great things of myself and great things of you as I seek to be your partner in transforming the world. In the name of Jesus the Healer. Amen.

+++

THE SEVENTEENTH DAY OF ADVENT

THIRSTING FOR GOD

As a deer longs for flowing streams, so my soul longs for you, O God.

> *My soul thirsts for God,*
> *for the living God.*
> *When shall I come and behold*
> *the face of God?*
> *My tears have been my food*
> *day and night,*
> *while people say to me continually,*
> *where is your God?"* (Psalm 42:1-3)

Old Testament scholar Walter Brueggemann speaks of three movements within the Psalms – orientation, disorientation, and new orientation – that reflect the nature of our relationship with God. Psalms of orientation reflect our gratitude for the beauty of the earth, the faithfulness of God, and personal and national success. Psalms of disorientation are sung when life falls apart: when in the midst of life, we find ourselves lost, without direction, and unable to experience the freshness of God's love. Psalms of new orientation emerge when once again God is real, the grief lifts, and we experience goodness of life. We can never go back to yesterday; but we can begin anew, perhaps wiser and stronger from the pain we have experienced, trusting that nothing, not even personal or national collapse, can separate us from the love of God.

Psalm 42 reflects a time of personal and community disorientation. Once, God's presence was real. Life was good and the future looked secure. Now, God seems absent, hidden by grief and uncertainty. "Where is God in this time of trial?" the Psalmist asks. Perhaps, the Psalmist is beginning to doubt the goodness and loving kindness of God. The Psalmist may be tempted to think it's all a sham anyway. But, to his and our amazement, the absence of God does not provoke disbelief, but a heart-felt, all-or-nothing, quest to rediscover God's presence.

As a deer longs for flowing streams,
so my soul longs for you, O God.
My soul thirsts for God,
for the living God.

This is not a Psalm for the impatient or faint-hearted. Just as a seed grows in darkness, dark moments may deepen our faith. Responding to adversity may build personal strength and courage. God does not bring the pain and sorrow to our lives; God wants us to live abundantly and joyfully. But, in the course of life, "stuff happens" that demolishes our well-planned futures. We may be left with nothing but the "thirst for God." What is powerful about this and other Psalms is that the Psalmist prays his or her fears, doubts, and complaints. The Psalmist brings her or his whole self to God.

Author Madeleine L'Engle was once asked following a lecture at a Christian college, "Do you believe in God without any doubts?" She responded, "I believe in God with all my doubts." When we bring our whole selves to God, including our questions, doubts, and pain, we may grow in spiritual maturity and sensitivity to the spiritual struggles of others.

In North America, the contemplative season of Advent is engulfed by the celebrative spirit of the Christmas season. Reflection is drowned out by tinny Christmas carols and consumerism. We are told that this is the season of joy and may feel despair because we simply are out of synch with the Christmas spirit and wonder what's wrong with us when we are struggling with grief, depression, and hopelessness. We want to experience the Christmas spirit, but life is flat and uninteresting. Psalm 42 is a testimony that even in the darkness of winter, faith trusts in the unseen. Quietly and often imperceptibly, God is at work in our lives, bringing healing and wholeness. Those who thirst for God will find refreshment. Those who bring their whole lives – trouble and joy – to God will find comfort. Those who despair will experience hope on the horizon. As the Psalmist prays:

Why are you cast down, O my soul, and why are you disquieted within me? Hope in God; for I shall again praise him, my help and my God.

Affirmation: I trust God's care in life's difficult moments. Help is on the way.

Action: Aware of your own experiences of loss and grief, take a moment to consider persons in your community who have lost loved ones in the past year or who are dealing with illnesses of body, mind, or spirit. If you feel comfortable, reach out with a card, e-mail, phone call, or visit. If this seems too bold for you, simply lift them up in prayer, asking that they feel God's nearness in the struggle and pain. Your prayers make a difference, and may enable them to experience a sense of hope.

Holy God, you know our joy and you know our pain. Help us to trust the growth that occurs in darkness. Help us to reach out for help or to reach out to comfort. Help us to trust our future and the future of our loved ones to your care. In the name of our Risen Savior. Amen.

THE EIGHTEENTH DAY OF ADVENT

NO HEALING IS TOO SMALL

When Jesus entered Peter's house, he saw his mother-in-law lying in bed with a fever; he touched her hand, and the fever left her, and she got up and began to serve him. That evening they brought to him many who were possessed by demons; and he cast out the spirits with a word, and cured all who were sick. This was to fulfill what had been spoken through the prophet Isaiah, "He took our infirmities and bore our diseases." (Matthew 8:14-17)

Have your ever gotten sick right before an important event? Even though you might just have had a cold, flu, or migraine, the illness threatened your plans. If so, you can relate to Peter's mother-in-law's experience. Her son-in-law's teacher was coming to dinner; he was a man of great power and charisma and she wanted to receive him with her best hospitality. In the first century, Peter's mother-in-law was the "woman of the house": running the house and greeting strangers was her vocation. Her illness was more than an inconvenience; it put her social vocation at risk. No doubt she was depressed at the thought of leaving the meal and hospitality to her daughter, regardless of how competent her daughter might have been.

Jesus recognizes her illness and its impact on her life, and makes it a priority to reach out to her. He touches her and restores her to health. In God's eyes – and our own – no healing is too small or large. God wants us to have abundant life and find joy in everyday responsibilities at home and work.

The healing, however, is not an end in itself. Peter's mother-in-law immediately gets up to serve the company. We are blessed to be a blessing. When we experience God's grace transforming our lives, we faithfully share that grace with others. We pass along the joy we have experienced, bringing joy and healing to others.

Affirmation: I am blessed to be a blessing. I share my good fortune with others.

Action: Take time to give thanks for the blessings you have received. Look for opportunities to share these blessings with others, especially the most vulnerable in your community.

Loving Parent, we ask for your healing touch. Restore us to wholeness of mind, body, spirit, and vocation, so that we might bless others through your love. In Christ's name. Amen.

+++

THE NINETEENTH DAY OF ADVENT

WE ARE CLOTHED IN CHRIST

As many of you as were baptized into Christ have clothed yourselves with Christ. There is no longer Jew or Greek, there is no longer slave or free, there is no longer male and female; for all of you are one in Christ Jesus. (Galatians 3:28-29)

The Benedictine religious community is known for its hospitality to strangers. In virtually every retreat house or monastery, you will see a plaque that proclaims, "See Christ in everyone." This is the essence of Paul's message to the church at Galatia, a congregation on the verge of splitting as a result of racial discrimination. Put briefly, the imposition of Jewish rules on Gentile Christians led these new Christians not only to be seen as second class members of the body of Christ; they also perceived themselves as second class Christians, who had to earn rather than accept God's love. Whereas dietary rules and male circumcision were norms in the Jewish Christian community, such practices diminished the cultural gifts of Gentile Christians and presented new converts with significant hardships, especially in terms of adult male circumcision.

The Apostle Paul will have nothing to do with such divisiveness. He sees the ritual requirements as undermining the freely-given, unconditional love of God. While God's grace may lead to personal transformation, grace itself comes freely, with no prior ritual or behavioral requirement.

Paul's solution to spiritual divisiveness and inequality is to proclaim our unity in Christ. Race, ethnicity, and gender matter, and contribute to the wondrous diversity of creation. They provide opportunities for growth rather than division. One in Christ, we are see all persons, male or female, Jew or Greek, slave or free, clothed in Christ Jesus and created in God's image.

The joyful hymns of Christmas, ready to burst forth in a few days, celebrate a grace that includes all of us. There are no outsiders to God's love. Everyone is valued as God's beloved child, calling us to see everyone with the eyes of Christ, holy in our diversity, affirmed in our uniqueness.

Affirmation: I see everyone, including myself, as God's beloved child.

Action: Take time to reflect on your community and congregation. Where do you see "outsiders?" Is anyone neglected or looked down upon? Consider prayerfully how you might respond to the divisions in your own heart and in your community. Ask God to reveal to you a pathway of reconciliation.

Loving God, who sees all of us as beloved, help us to become channels of grace to everyone we meet. Seeing Christ's presence in ourselves, help us to see and bring forth Christ's presence in others. Amen.

+++

THE TWENTIETH DAY OF ADVENT

GOD'S SPIRIT IS IN OUR HEARTS

But when the fullness of time had come, God sent his Son, born of a woman, born under the law, in order to redeem those who were under the law, so that we might receive adoption as children. And because you are children, God has sent the Spirit of his Son into our hearts, crying, "Abba! Father!" So you are no

> *longer a slave but a child, and if a child then also an heir, through God.* (Galatians 4:4-7)

Have you ever considered the possibility that God is constantly speaking to you? Not necessarily in words, but in inclinations, hunches, dreams, and intuitions. In Romans 8, the Apostle Paul describes God's Spirit as our deepest reality. According to Paul, "When we cry 'Abba, Father!' it is the Spirit bearing witness that we are children of God." Moreover, Paul believes that God's "Spirit intercedes for us in sighs too deep for words."

Most of the time, we fail to hear God's voice. It's drowned out by the many voices in our environment and our own inner experience. When we take time to pause, we may hear a divine melody echoing in our hearts and minds. It may not come to us in words, but may give us the calm reassurance that God is moving in our lives and that, as the British mystic Julian of Norwich proclaims, "all shall be well and all shall be well and all manner of thing shall be well." Hearing the voice of God within our lives alerts us to our deepest identity. Our lives are not purposeless or random. We are not expendable. We are God's children and God wants us to have abundant life. Open to the gentle whispers of the Spirit, we see God's presence in all of God's beloved children, and bless them as we are blessed.

Affirmation: God is constantly communicating with me. I experience God in both the conscious and unconscious mind.

Action: Recognizing that I am one of God's beloved children, I commit myself to treating everyone I meet as a beloved child of God. I make it my responsibility to support the well-being of God's children in my neighborhood through healthy encounters and programs that benefit the most vulnerable members of our community. I explore ways to support the well-being of children of God across the country and in other lands through advocacy that cuts across party lines and generosity to programs that serve vulnerable persons across the globe.

Whispering God, incline my ear to your voice and my senses to your presence. Help me to see your glory in the smallest things and live a life of healing and blessing in Christ's name. Amen.

+++

THE TWENTY FIRST DAY OF ADVENT

RESTORING OUR SPIRITS

Restore us, O Lord God of hosts; let your face shine, that we may be saved. (Psalm 80:19)

Many of us need restoration. We know that we can never go back to the way things used to be, nor, frankly, do we want to. We have experienced the pain and disappointment of broken dreams, ambiguous childhoods, personal trauma, professional failure, relational breakups, and physical illness; we also recognize that we can't take back words spoken and deeds done. We need healing and restoration; we need, as the apostle Paul proclaims, to become new creations. Faith is an adventure of the spirit. Each day brings new possibilities and new ways of living our lives. Our scriptures are bold in proclaiming that:

- God's mercies are new every morning.
- God is constantly doing a new thing.
- We can become a new creation.
- We don't have to be conformed to the past, we can experience transformed lives.

The challenge, for many of us, is taking these first steps in Advent adventuring. Advent presents us with the difference between who we are and what we can become. This difference, radical though it may be, is intended to inspire rather than shame us. Whether we know it or not, God is working in our lives; God's gentle providence is providing us with pathways toward the future in terms of insights, dreams, and encounters. Christ is knocking at the door of our lives, ready to give us all we need to move forward, if we crack the door open and invite him in.

There are many ways to respond to God's call to restoration and new creation. Every adventure begins with a small step and that small step involves prayer and openness to change. It may involve a small step out of your comfort zone to attempt a new behavior or reconcile with another person. There is always a risk to every adventure, but without the risk, there can be no abundant living. God calls us to take "baby steps" toward the future, trusting that once we open the door, we will discover Christ will be our companion on the journey forward.

Affirmation: I open my heart and soul to God's call to restoration and adventure.

Action: The spiritual journey begins with prayer, involving a simple request that you can phrase in your own way: "I open the door to my life. Give me courage to the first steps in healing and restoration. Show me path, and bring events and persons into my life to help me move forward. Thank you for your abundant grace and loving energy." As insights emerge, take a chance by following the wisdom you receive. When God calls us forward, God gives us energy and insight enough for each step of the adventure.

Adventurous Companion, guide my spirit and my feet. I open to your wisdom as it leads me to horizons of restoration and healing. In Jesus' name. Amen.

+++

THE TWENTY SECOND DAY OF ADVENT

GOD SPEAKS IN DREAMS AND INTUITIONS

Now the birth of Jesus the Messiah took place in this way. When his mother Mary had been engaged to Joseph, but before they lived together, she was found to be with child from the Holy Spirit. Her husband

> *Joseph, being a righteous man and unwilling to expose her to public disgrace, planned to dismiss her quietly. But just when he had resolved to do this, an angel of the Lord appeared to him in a dream and said, "Joseph, son of David, do not be afraid to take Mary as your wife, for the child conceived in her is from the Holy Spirit. She will bear a son, and you are to name him Jesus, for he will save his people from their sins."*
> (Matthew 1:18-21)

Advent invites us to adventures of the spirit in which we discover God on every pathway and in every encounter. Many people identify faith solely with doctrinal beliefs and intellectual propositions. While imaginative reflection on the great creeds of the church (Apostles, Nicene) can provide a framework for living, God also comes to us through the unconscious mind, through which God speaks in "sighs too deep for words."

In the past century, Sigmund Freud and Carl Jung have described the importance of dreams in psychological well-being. Going far beyond his teacher Freud, Jung asserted that dreams can reveal divine wisdom and help us understand God's calling in our lives. In today's reading, the reliable yet radically unsettled Joseph receives a life-transforming dream.

God's angelic messenger, working through the unconscious mind, tells him that he and his family are blessed. The angel assures him that all will be well for Joseph, for Mary is bearing is God's gift to humankind. God speaks in dreams and Joseph listens and changes his course, accepting Mary as his wife, despite the strange circumstances of her pregnancy.

Our dreams can reveal paths untaken, wounds unhealed, and adventures luring us forward. Take time to reflect on your dreams, prayerfully as well as analytically. Could God be giving you a word of guidance in a particular dream? What would happen if you took your dreams seriously as revealing divine wisdom?

Affirmation: God speaks to me in dreams, insights, hunches, and encounters.

Action: Ask God to reveal God's wisdom for your life and then commit yourself to seeing the whole of your life as opportunity to receive guidance from the Holy Spirit. Take your dreams seriously and perhaps share your dreams with a wise spiritual guide. You may discover great wisdom and insights into neglected parts of your life or pathways toward God's own dreams for you.

God of wisdom and light, help me to receive your guidance in whatever media it is presented to me. Let me trust your wisdom, moving forward gently with your as my guide and companion. In Jesus' name. Amen.

+++

THE TWENTY THIRD DAY OF ADVENT

I REJOICE IN GOD'S PRESENCE

My soul magnifies God, and my spirit rejoices in God my Savior....God has filled the hungry with good things, and sent the rich away empty. (Luke 1:46, 53)

Mary's Magnificat is one of the great hymns of scripture. A song of joy from an unexpectedly pregnant woman has throughout the ages inspired social reformers as well oppressed persons to claim God's affirmation of their quest for equality and justice. Mary's hymn is not for the faint-hearted or those who invoke "we've always done it this way." She challenges us to become pregnant with God's creative transformation and share in God's birthing of a brand new world.

Mary is a surprising prophet. The recipient of an angelic visitor, and an unwed mother, she models what it means to be open to God's vision for our lives. Utterly powerless, she becomes a vehicle of God's power. While some traditions assert that Mary is unique among women, insofar as she was conceived without the taint of original sin, I believe that Mary's uniqueness is found in her full humanness in all its beauty and imperfection. Separating her from us by some ideal of perfection makes her affirmative response to God's call irrelevant to our human condition. If Mary was preprogramed and predestined to say "yes," her willingness would be automatic and not an act of faithful discipleship. Instead, Mary responded to God's call to give birth to the Christ child with all her perplexity and uncertainty. She embarked on an adventure with no guarantees of success and no clear destination. Mary's "yes" put her at risk physically and socially. At the very least, if Joseph had not come forward, she would have been disgraced as an adulteress. She might even have been subject to death by stoning. Yet, Mary said "yes."

As I ponder the story of Jesus' conception, the main point is that Mary said "yes" to God's call in all its surprising possibility. No doubt her life of commitment to God, reflected in an unusual openness to God, prepared her for Gabriel's visitation. But, still she had the freedom to say "no" to God's extravagant invitation. We don't know if she was the first young woman Gabriel asked; but what we do know is that she was the first to say "yes" and her "yes" to God transformed history and opened humankind to God's vision of salvation.

In the Hebraic tradition, spirituality, politics, and economics are interrelated. Mary's hymn describes a God who gives good things to the hungry and poor. God reaches out to the neediest among us and challenges the wealthy whose largesse is acquired dishonestly and unjustly. God also loves the wealthy, but Mary's hymn challenges the "haves" to use their wealth for the benefit of society's most vulnerable members.

As you reflect on Mary's hymn, where are you called to say "yes" to God? What would it look like for you to "magnify" God in praise?

Affirmation: I give glory to God by my words and actions. I open myself to God's extravagant invitations. I take a chance on God by doing something new and creative.

Action: In the spirit of Mary's hymn, consider where you might choose to be God's companion in bringing good things to the hungry and poor. This might mean that you become involved in an advocacy group such as Bread for the World. It might also lead you to support international programs such as World Vision or Church World Service. Closer to home you might directly support the most economically vulnerable persons in your community by volunteering at Habitat for Humanity building project, preparing meals at a soup kitchen, making casseroles for the local shelter, collecting school supplies for underprivileged children, or serving breakfast at the overnight shelter.

Loving God, help us hear the cries of the poor. Let us follow Mary in saying "yes" to your adventure of Shalom. Let us give birth to something beautiful in recognition of God's great gifts to us. In Christ's name. Amen.

THE CHRISTMAS SEASON

ADVENTURES IN INCARNATIONAL LIVING

Christmas is the season for children. Each day, the pace quickens as we live in anticipation of presents under the tree and a visit from Santa Claus. Christmas can also be a season of anxiety for shoppers and for small children. I remember the Christmas that almost did not come. All my childhood, we had spent Christmas Eve and morning at our home in King City, California. But, the year of my sixth Christmas, my family was planning to drive south to Los Angeles on Christmas Eve and spend Christmas Day with my aunt and uncle in Los Angeles. The idea that we weren't going to be home on Christmas Day filled me with anxiety. Would Santa Claus come to my aunt and uncle's home? How would Santa know to find me and my brother? Would we get any presents at all?

As Christmas Eve approached, I was really anxious. My Dad, the local Baptist pastor, had to record a meditation for the local station that evening and so my brother and I along with our Mom went to Mrs. Cline's home for hot chocolate and cookies. When my Dad stopped to pick us up, the car was packed and ready to go. He surprised us by saying, "I think we should stop home to use the bathroom and make sure we didn't forget anything." That surprised me because Dad always wanted to hit the road at the earliest possible moment.

The moment my Dad opened the door, my heart was filled with joy: the tree was ablaze in light and surrounded by mountains of packages. Christmas had come! It didn't matter the time or the place, Santa would remember us.

That's the story of the incarnation. Wherever we go, and now far we've strayed, God will remember us, and search everywhere just to give us the gift of Christmas. The story of the first Christmas is breathtaking in its simplicity: an unexpected pregnancy, a perplexed father, a loving mother, homelessness, and the callous indifference of political powers. The Savior of the World is born in a humble manger, taking his first breath among an innkeeper's domestic animals. This is the story of one small child, born in apparent obscurity. But, that manger is every house and everywhere. Christ is born where we least expect it, and on the darkest night a light shines, giving guidance for every traveler's journey.

Once upon a time, a star shined in the heavens, guiding magi from a faraway land and that star still shines, noticed or noticed, whenever God shows up in our lives. When we look upon a star, we will find ourselves on an unexpected journey, with magi, shepherds, and expectant parents as our companions.

In describing Christmas, one of my spiritual teachers Howard Thurman reflects: "The mood of Christmas – what is it? It is the quickening of the presence of other human beings into whose lives a precious part of one's own has been released. It is a memory of other days when into one's life an angel appeared spreading a halo over an ordinary moment or commonplace event. It is an iridescence of sheer delight that bathes one's whole being with something more wonderful than words can ever tell."[3]

One night changed the world. Twelve days can change your life. Listen for the angels. With George Bailey, you may find an angel watching over you when you're ready to give up, and then discover "it's a wonderful life." With Ebenezer Scrooge, you may discover that in spite of the past, your heart can break right open to let love in. You may not expect it, but Christmas is here, "Joy to the world the Lord has come."

---

[3] Howard Thurman, *The Mood of Christmas xiii* (Richmond, IN: Friends United Press, 1973)

THE BIRTH OF JESUS – CHRISTMAS EVE

A SURPRISING INCARNATION

> *In that region there were shepherds living in the fields, keeping watch over their flock by night. Then an angel of the Lord stood before them, and the glory of the Lord shone around them, and they were terrified. But the angel said to them, 'Do not be afraid; for see—I am bringing you good news of great joy for all the people: to you is born this day in the city of David a Saviour, who is the Messiah, the Lord.* (Luke 2:8-10)

> *The people who walked in darkness have seen a great light.* (Isaiah 9:2)

The Christmas story is always an unexpected surprise. If we bracket our familiarity with the story for a moment, the story becomes even more surprising. Imagine God's revelation coming to a working class girl and her carpenter fiancé; the angelic choir singing to unkempt, minimum wage workers, profiled by the authorities as shiftless, smelly, and street-wise; and the birth happening in a cave, cluttered with hay, tools, chickens, and a cow. In our age of celebrity in which people are famous simply because they make news with extravagant spending, substance abuse, and bad behavior, the notion that God's most significant revelation would occur among the poor and powerless is an affront to our sensibilities. But, people at the margins of society are often the most receptive to God's revelations. In their utter powerlessness, they know they need a miracle. With no buffers between them and homelessness and poverty, they know they can't make it on their own and yearn for the coming of a new age. A child is an image of hope and the promise of a better future – for them and perhaps for us.

Shocked out of their wits at the angelic visitation, the shepherds need to be comforted. "Don't be afraid," the angel assures them, "I have good news for you. Help is on the way. God is coming visibly to your world." The coming of the light can be disorienting for the shepherds and us; it can also liberate us to dream again. As the prophet Isaiah proclaimed several centuries before Jesus' birth, "The people who walked in darkness have seen a great light." The days of darkness can become days of awe when we discover God in our midst. The shepherds run to the stable and give glory to the newborn child. From here on, everything will be changed. Still at the lowest rung of the social ladder, still trying to make ends meet, the shepherds have new hope for the present and future. They discover that regardless of what others think about them, they are God's own children, the salt that gives savor to life. God is with us: we matter to God and God has heard and responded to our heart's deepest desires. We can live again.

The Christmas stories should astound us as well. We have much to fear and we need angelic reassurance that "all shall be well and all shall be well and all manner of thing shall be well." (Julian of Norwich) We need a light to guide us to places where God comes alive in our midst. We need a pathway to the future. That's the spirit of Christmas: you are beloved, surrounded by God's light, and can venture forth to tomorrow with hope in your heart and song on lips. "Joy to the world, our Christ has come!" Joy is coming to you!

Affirmation: I open to God's birthing in unexpected places. I open to God's birthing in my life.

Action: As children, we lived in great anticipation of the coming of Christmas. Whether we opened the presents on Christmas Eve or in the morning, we knew that there would be surprises and we could hardly wait. Throughout the day, open to God's surprising presence in your life and make your life a surprising gift to another through a kind word, an unexpected call or e-mail or visit to someone in need. God is with us in the adventures of the Christmas season.

Holy Child, in the darkness, you give us light. In confusion, you give us direction. In uncertainty, you give us hope. Help us, like the shepherds, to be filled with awe that inspires us to seek the Christ in life's most unexpected places and share the Christ with those who have been rendered hopeless and fearful by the pain and violence of the world. In Jesus' name. Amen.

+++

CHRISTMAS DAY – THE BIRTH OF JESUS

CHRIST IS BORN US!

So the shepherds went with haste and found Mary and Joseph, and the child lying in the manger. When they saw this, they made known what had been told them about this child; and all who heard it were amazed at what the shepherds told them. But Mary treasured all these words and pondered them in her heart. (Luke 2:17-19)

> *The light shines in the darkness, and the darkness did not overcome it.…The true light, which enlightens everyone, was coming into the world.* (John 1: 5, 9)

Christmas joins the intimate and the ultimate. The birth of Jesus is intensely personal. Every parent can relate to the wonder of her or his child's birth. The whole universe, for a moment, is localized in the birthing room. Although it has been repeated several billion times, this particular birth is unique in all the cosmos. This particular child is born, reflecting the fullness of God's creativity, as her or she comes to life, as the poet Wordsworth claims:

> Trailing clouds of glory…
> From God who is our home.

Jesus' birth is so normal, and yet holy in its ordinariness. An early theologian, Iranaeus, proclaimed that the glory of God is a person who is fully alive. While we may forget our divine origins and the divine image that is our deepest reality, Jesus grew in wisdom and stature, living fully and inviting us to become fully alive ourselves.

On that first Christmas, the divine and human danced together, one in spirit and flesh. The light shined in the darkness of human life, bringing light to every mother's child. Today that light shines in each of us, ready to burst forth when we open to God's movements in our lives. You are the light of the world. In Christ, let God's light shine through you. Let your light shine. Give light to all around.

Affirmation: God's light is shining in and through me. Christ is being born in my life.

Action: John's Gospel says that God's light shines in everyone. Throughout the day, look for God's light shining in unexpected places and persons. Pray for ways to bring forth that light in the people around you, loved ones, friends, and strangers.

Giver of light and life, whose light shines in all of us, help us to glow with your loving presence. Help us to see and share your light. Help us to be lights in the darkness, bringing healing wherever we go. In Christ's name. Amen.

+++

THE SECOND DAY OF CHRISTMAS

GOD CARES FOR US INSPITE OF OUR SIN

> *Jerusalem, Jerusalem, the city that kills the prophets and stones those who are sent to it! How often have I desired to gather your children together as a hen gathers her brood under her wings, and you were not willing!* (Matthew 23:37)

If only the world took on the shape of Christmas! Alas, and how unsettling it is, the day after Christmas is not just Boxing Day, it is the Feast of St. Stephen the Martyr, stoned for his faithfulness to the Risen Christ. (Acts 7:1-60) Like his Savior Jesus, the dying Stephen asked God to forgive his persecutors. Like a mother hen, God wants to protect and nurture us. But, humans – like the people of Jerusalem – often prefer their own individual agendas to God's loving vision for everyone. Still, God seeks our salvation. God wants to embrace us in loving arms, and guide us toward what is best for us and the world.

God never gives up on us. We may hide from God but God still runs after us, willing to suffer that we might find our place in God's eternal realm – right now and forever more. This is the promise of Christmas – God with us, knowing our personal and community conditions and working within the concrete realities of life to heal, empower, and transform us. Hallelujah! God's light shines in us and guides our path to the Holy Child!

Affirmation: God cares for us regardless of our past. God searches after us, always ready to welcome us home.

Action: We have received grace. Our vocation is to share this grace with others. In the spirit of St. Stephen the Martyr, let us examine our hearts, noting where we are alienated from others, and taking the pathway of forgiveness and reconciliation, first, in our hearts and, then, if warranted, in person. If forgiveness is too painful either in terms of reaching out or if the person you need to forgive has died, simply place the pain in God's hands, asking God to do what you cannot do at the moment, to make reconciliation and to heal your memories and sense of alienation. (To be clear, certain events may be too painful to deal with on our own. In that case, make an appointment with a trusted spiritual leader or counselor. Forgiveness does not mean accepting bad behavior or letting others take advantage of you; it may mean the "tough love" of placing limits and setting boundaries on others' behaviors for your and their well-being.)

Jesus, I place my pain and alienation in your care. Heal my broken heart, free me from the burden of the past, and transform my memories. Help me forgive those who have hurt me and help me advocate for those who are traumatized by the actions of others. In Christ's name. Amen.

+++

THE THIRD DAY OF CHRISTMAS, FEAST OF JOHN THE EVANGELIST

IT IS ALL GOOD!

In the beginning when God created the heavens and the earth, the earth was a formless void and darkness covered the face of the deep, while a wind from God swept over the face of the waters. Then God said, 'Let there be light'; and there was light. And God saw that the light was good; and God separated the light from the darkness. God called the light Day, and the darkness he called Night. And there was evening and there was morning, the first day…..Then God said,

> *'Let us make humankind in our image, according to our likeness…..in the image of God he created them; male and female he created them.* (Genesis 1:1-5, 26-27)

Although the words of the Genesis creation story have often been used to justify a literal six day, twenty four hour, creation of the universe, less than ten thousand years ago, this image of divine creativity was hardly the intent of the Hebraic storytellers and wisdom givers. They were more interested in the rock of ages than the age of rocks! Unlike many other creation stories circulating in the Middle East, the Hebraic creation story focuses on the wisdom and generosity of God, the goodness of creation, and the partnership of God and humankind. In contrast to the creation myths of its neighbors, the image of God portrayed in the Genesis story describes God as wanting our success and encouraging our agency, rather than being threatened by human achievements.

John the Gospel writer is celebrated today because he, like the authors of the Genesis creation story, saw human life as part of a great cosmic adventure. God is present in the first breath of creation, bringing beauty and order to that which is unformed, and God moves through history, guided the creation of stars, planets, plants, sea creatures, birds, mammals, and eventually human beings. God's creative wisdom brings forth life in all its forms, working with creation as an artist works with her or his palette or a writer works with words. And it is good!

God's creation is good: the heavens are good, the flora and fauna are good, human life is good, your body is good, and, in God's eyes, your creativity is good. Life is good. There is no need to escape this world or long for heaven. This world itself is heavenly if we open our senses to its beauty and take our role as God's companions in the ongoing creation and healing of our planet.

Male and female are created in God's image. Genesis proclaims the original goodness of creation. Long before the appearance of human sin, we were created to be God's companions, gardeners and artists of creation. Despite our imperfection, God's image still is present as our deepest reality. The God who creates both transcends and embraces gender: there is no male or female superiority in Genesis. The divine relationship with the world affirms the male and the female in all their glorious unity and diversity. Today, the Genesis story invites us to love God in the world of the flesh, in the flight of an eagle, in the waters of the ocean, and in the faces of our human and non-human companions. It is good.

Affirmation: I am created in God's image. God's goodness defines who I am.

Action: God calls us to be companions in the creative process. Creation continues and despite the threats to the good Earth, we can still claim our role in the healing of creation. Consider what you can do to bring beauty to the earth. In light of God's continuing creativity, how can you be a gardener or artist of creation, supporting life in all its diverse forms? How can you be God's partner in healing the Earth?

Creative and Loving Wisdom, we thank you for your artistry, for the universe in its vastness and the beauty of our little planet. Help us to live in gratitude and amazement at the beauty of the Earth and help us to claim our role as your companions in healing our planet. In Christ's name. Amen.

+++

Bruce G. Epperly

THE FOURTH DAY OF CHRISTMAS, REMEMBERING THE HOLY INNOCENTS

PROTECTING THE CHILDREN

When Herod saw that he had been tricked by the wise men, he was infuriated, and he sent and killed all the children in and around Bethlehem who were two years old or under, according to the time that he had learned from the wise men. Then was fulfilled what had been spoken through the prophet Jeremiah: "A voice was heard in Ramah, wailing and loud lamentation, Rachel weeping for her children; she refused to be consoled, because they are no more." (Matthew 2:16-18)

Today's reading should be labeled "parental advisory – this story contains violence." I hesitated to add this passage to our text – after all, it is so depressing - but the realities of life and Jesus' incarnation compel me to affirm the joyful message of Christmas carols and the tragic reality of violence against the most innocent and vulnerable, the children.

Shortly after Jesus' birth, Joseph has another dream, warning him to take Mary and their newborn child to Egypt. The scriptures remind us that Joseph, Mary, and Jesus were political refugees, and like many persons today, fled from one country to another to find safety and a better life. Tragically, Herod massacred the remaining toddlers and babies of Bethlehem.

As a grandparent, I have made a commitment to nurture and protect my own grandchildren. I will do almost anything to insure their survival and flourishing, including sacrificing my own security and well-being. I have also made a commitment to care for all the other grandchildren of the world, whether they be school children in my hometown of Centerville, Massachusetts, insuring that they have adequate school supplies and safe environments, children in North American inner cities and Appalachia, and infants and youngsters in Somalia and Uganda.[4]

It has been said that when you save one soul, you save the world. Today's reading challenges us to begin saving the lives of children and treasuring their innocence in a world of violent images in the media, inadequate diets, substandard schools, unsafe neighborhoods, and political genocide. The task is overwhelming, but one child at a time, it can be done. Remember someone reached out to Jesus' family;

---

[4] For more on the spirituality of grand parenting, see Bruce Epperly, *Letters to My Grandson: Wisdom from a Fresh Perspective* (Gonzales, FL, 2013)

someone found them a home and helped Joseph secure employment. They were "aliens" but someone sacrificed so that Jesus could survive and then thrive and live to become our Savior, Healer, and Teacher. Let us bless the children.

Affirmation: I commit myself to saving the world one child at a time.

Action: Take time to explore the challenges children face in your neighborhood. How can you and your congregation help to improve the schools in your town? How can you advocate for safe havens for children after school and on weekends? How can we provide support for young mothers and fathers as they raise their children? Consider also supporting an international program whose focus is families and children such as World Vision, Save the Children, UNICEF, Church World Service, or the Christian Children's Fund. The world is saved one child at a time.

Holy God, whose Beloved Son blessed the children, help us bless the children of our church and community, and the children of the world. Help us work for a world in which the sounds of children playing and laughing fill the air, and all children have homes, food, and love. In Christ's Name. Amen.

+++

THE FIFTH DAY OF CHRISTMAS

GOD'S GRACIOUS LOVE SAVES US

I will recount the gracious deeds of the LORD, *the praiseworthy acts of the* LORD, *because of all that the* LORD *has done for us, and the great favor to the house of Israel that he has shown them according to his mercy, according to the abundance of his steadfast love....but his presence that saved them; in his love and in his pity he redeemed them; he lifted them up and carried them all the days of old.* (Isaiah 63:7, 9)

The Hebraic meaning of Jesus' name is "God saves." This is the point of the incarnation of God in time and space. The One who creates the universe in all its wonder is also the source of healing and wholeness. Our lives and the historical process are ambiguous in nature: every advance creates the possibility of greater evil along with greater good. We need spiritual wisdom to keep us on the path of life – to choose life rather than death and good rather than evil.

The passage from Isaiah describes God's restoration of fallen Israel. As a result of its turning from God toward the gods of greed and materialism, the nation of Israel is overwhelmed by Babylon and Assyria. Despite its deeds of injustice, God is willing to give Israel a new beginning. God is also willing to give us a new beginning. If we just open the door to Jesus, we will experience unexpected calm, energy, and wisdom. We will discover that regardless of the past, God has not given up on us – or anyone else – and is ready to give us everything we need to flourish in the future.

As we prepare to say "goodbye" to 2013, we can let go of the past and awaken to God's new creation, moving in our lives. We can open to the new possibilities God is offering to us. God is on our side and wants us to have abundant life. It is ours for the claiming, for God's vision for us is always more than we ask and imagine. (Ephesians 3:20)

Affirmation: I let go of the past and open to God's future possibilities.

Action: As you look back on 2013, what aspects of the past year limit you? What things do you need to let go of? What burdens do you bear? Take time to ask God to help you free yourself from the past so that you can awaken to new adventures in 2014.

God of all seasons, the heaviness of the past often bears down on us. Help us to become new creations, free to follow your visions for tomorrow, free to become your companions in creating a new future for ourselves and the world. In Jesus' name. Amen.

+++

THE SIXTH DAY OF CHRISTMAS

WE ARE BEING RENEWED EVERYDAY

So we do not lose heart. Even though our outer nature is wasting away, our inner nature is being renewed day by day. For this slight momentary affliction is preparing us for an eternal weight of glory beyond all measure, because we look not at what can be seen but at what cannot be seen; for what can be seen is temporary, but what cannot be seen is eternal. (2 Corinthians 5:16-18)

Reality is more than meets the eye. Each person is more than meets the eye. When we are tempted to focus on the limitations of age, gender, and health, Paul reminds us, from the vantage point of his prison cell that God is working within our spirits, inspiring us to grow in spite of life's challenges.

The biblical tradition sees humans as a dynamic interplay of mind, body, spirit, emotions, and relationships. It is easy to focus on the obvious, flesh and blood, and its inherent mortality and neglect the spiritual that shares in God's everlasting life. We need to see beyond the surface of life to honor the everlasting in ourselves and others. Everyone we meet has been given God's everlasting spirit and deserves to be treated accordingly. We have been given God's everlasting spirit and deserve to honor ourselves as created in God's image, regardless of our age, health, or physical capabilities. As Paul proclaims, "what can be seen is temporary, but what cannot be seen is eternal." What would it mean for you to see yourself as created in God's image and sharing in God's everlasting life? What would it mean to see others in the same way? How would it change your values and vision?

Our vision of everlasting life is not intended to devalue our bodies or earthly life, but invest them with holiness as the realm in which we are given the opportunity to learn our destiny as God's beloved. The incarnation is a constant reminder that everyday life is permeated with eternity and every moment can be a revelation of God.

Affirmation: Regardless of my age or physical condition, I share in God's everlasting life.

Action: Recognizing that the reality of each of us is more than meets the eye, make the commitment to treat everyone as a spiritual as well as physical being. Look for the holiness in others and help bring it out by acts of respect and support.

Loving and Creative God, your wisdom and holiness permeate all things. Give us eyes to see your presence in all things and challenge us to become your companions in helping others discover their destiny in your everlasting adventure. In Christ's name. Amen.

+++

THE SEVENTH DAY OF CHRISTMAS

MORTAL, YET DIVINE

When I look at your heavens, the work of your fingers, the moon and the stars that you have established; what are human beings that you are mindful of them,

> *mortals that you care for them? Yet you have made them a little lower than God, and crowned them with glory and honor.* (Psalm 8:3-5)

A Jewish wisdom saying counsels that we should have a note in each of our pockets. The first note should read, "You are dust," while the second should assert, "For you the universe was made." This is the insight of Psalm 8: long before the discovery of the big bang, the multi-billion galaxy universe, and the immense cosmic journey of nearly fourteen billion years, the Psalmist recognized the precarious nature of our planet, ourselves, and everything we love. We appear, as Walker Pearcy notes, to be "lost in the universe." We are hardly a speck in interstellar space. Our planet's life forms are at the mercy of asteroids and solar flares. Astonished by the immensity and grandeur of the universe, the Psalmist wonders if we matter at all. But, then, the Psalmist realizes that humankind shares in God's image. We are called to be creators, following the pattern of the Creative Wisdom that brought forth the universe. We are mortals and we must die, but we also share in God's everlasting life and are endowed with imagination, ingenuity, and creativity. We have a vocation to be God's companions in tending for creation on our small but beautiful planet.

The incarnation of God in human flesh means

that this life, our life, is filled with the grandeur of God. As the prophetic mystic Isaiah exclaimed in reflecting on his encounter with God in the Jerusalem Temple, "the whole earth is full of God's glory!" (Isaiah 6:3) Incarnation is an invitation to think big and do great things, for God is counting on our efforts to heal this good Earth.

Affirmation: I share in God's everlasting life. I live as one whose life is in God's everlasting care.

Action: For personal examination, consider the question: What am I afraid of? Then, ponder how you would respond to your fears if you knew you were in God's everlasting care and that in Christ, you have everlasting life in companionship with God. Death is real, but death cannot defeat God or wrest you from God's care? What bold act might you do in response to God's victorious love for you?

Everlasting God, I trust my life to your care. My times are in your hands. I am forever safe in your presence. Help me to be courageous, and faithful to your quest for Shalom, knowing that nothing in life can separate me from your love. In Christ's name. Amen.

+++

THE EIGHTH DAY OF CHRISTMAS, NEW YEAR'S DAY,

THE FEAST OF THE NAME OF JESUS GODLY POWER

Let this mind be in you, which was also in Christ Jesus: Who, being in the form of God, thought it not robbery to be equal with God: But made himself of no reputation, and took upon him the form of a servant, and was made in the likeness of men: And being found in fashion as a human, he humbled himself, and became obedient unto death, even the death of the cross. Wherefore God also hath highly exalted him, and given him a name which is above every name: That at the name of Jesus every knee should bow, of things in heaven, and things in earth, and things under the earth; And that every tongue should confess that Jesus Christ is Lord, to the glory of God the Father. (Philippians 2:5-11)

Many scholars believe that Paul's words from Philippians 2 are an adaptation of an early Christian hymn, describing Christ's work and ultimate victory over the powers of evil. This is a good message for New Year's Day. We need guidance regarding how to live our lives, and Jesus is, according to the Apostle Paul, the one true model for healthy and faithful living. We are to have "the mind of Christ" individually and as communities. We are to see the world with the eyes of Jesus, make decisions guided by his wisdom, and reach out with the hands of Jesus. Paul's Philippian listeners would have thought of two kinds of power as they heard these words. The first image would be that of Caesar, who ruled by violence and threat. Caesar's power was unilateral and unbending, "my way or the highway" compulsion. We bow our knees to such power in fear or to secure gain from the potentate. The second image is that of Jesus, whose power took him to the Cross, who lived as one of us, and welcomed the lost and broken as full participants in God's realm of Shalom. Jesus' power is healing power that gives power to others. Jesus never threatened or coerced. Although he often warned that certain behaviors would lead to painful consequences, he sought to expand freedom and creativity. He looked for companions, not slaves, to continue and grow his ministry. Every knee bows to Jesus out of love and gratitude, and then rises up ready to go forward in his mission of healing and Shalom.

As a new year begins, let us have the mind of Christ, loving, welcoming, healing, and embracing. Let us use our gifts and power to bring out the gifts of others in the quest for God's realm "on earth as it is in heaven."

Affirmation: I have the mind of Christ. I see the world and respond to daily life through Christ's eyes.

Action: In the spirit of Paul's image of the mind of Christ, consider the quality of your personal relationships. Do you act relationally, taking into consideration the gifts and feelings of others? Do you tend to make unilateral decisions that disempower and disregard the gifts of others? In what ways might you embrace the mind of Christ? Today make a commitment to listen and respond to others, seeking to encourage their creativity and personal growth.

Loving God, help me to see the world through your eyes. Help me to honor my own gifts and encourage the gifts of others. Open to your blessings, I seek to bless the world and those around me. In Christ's name. Amen.

THE NINTH DAY OF CHRISTMAS

FINDING A HEART OF WISDOM

In Gibeon the LORD *appeared to Solomon in a dream by night: and God said, Ask what I shall give thee......Give therefore thy servant an understanding heart to judge thy people, that I may discern between good and bad: for who is able to judge this thy so great a people?* (I Kings 3:5, 9)

Jesus once asked a sight-impaired man, "What do you want me to do for you?" (Mark 10:46-52) With a similar intent, God addresses Solomon, as Solomon begins his rule of Israel, "Ask what I shall give thee." Solomon has lots of options: great wealth, military power, world conquest. He chooses the most important thing: an understanding heart, a heart of wisdom, to perform his vocation as leader.

How would you respond to Jesus' question to the sight-impaired Bartimaeus, "What do you want me to do for you?" What would you say if God addressed you, "Ask what I shall give you"? Your answer will give you a sense of your current values. It will reveal what theologian Paul Tillich calls your "ultimate concern," the most important thing in your life. How do you evaluate your response? With more reflection, what changes might you make? How do your values shape your daily life?

The Christmas season reminds us that God is willing to give us more than we can ask or imagine – that God seeks abundant life – in the balance of love for others and love for ourselves. God is on our side and invites us to be on adventures of creativity and love. When we open to God's vision of what we can become, we are amazed to discover how wonderful life can be.

Affirmation: I seek a heart of wisdom.

Action: Prayerfully go through the day opening to the gifts God is preparing to give you. In every situation, ask God to give you a heart of wisdom and help you discern your deepest desires for that particular event or encounter.

Giver of life and love, grant me a heart of wisdom. Help me discern your calling in every situation that I might be faithful to you and your kingdom. In Christ's name. Amen.

+++

THE TENTH DAY OF CHRISTMAS

THIN PLACES

And Jacob went out from Beersheba, and went toward Haran. And he lighted upon a certain place, and tarried there all night, because the sun was set; and he took of the stones of that place, and put them for his pillows, and lay down in that place to sleep. And he dreamed, and behold a ladder set up on the earth, and the top of it reached to heaven: and behold the angels of God ascending and descending on it....And Jacob awakened out of his sleep, and he said, Surely the LORD is in this place; and I knew it not. (Genesis 28:10-12, 16)

The Celtic tradition celebrates the reality of thin places, where heaven and earth meet. While these places may be sacred groves or windswept seashores, they can emerge any and everywhere, when we open our eyes to the ever-present God.

Jacob discovers a thin place that transforms his life. Weary from a day's travel, Jacob camps in a deserted place, far from his flocks, family, and herdsmen. Alone, and facing his past as a trickster and crafty (dare we say, unscrupulous) businessman, he falls into a deep sleep and dreams of a ladder of angels, reaching up from earth to heaven. What is strange about this ladder is that the angels ascend before they return to Earth. Could it be that Earth is filled with divine messengers? Could it be that Earth is a holy place, chock-full with divinity for those whose senses are alert? Perhaps, we don't need to "go" to heaven to find God; heaven is already here and ready to open the doors to a life of blessing.

In his dream, Jacob receives a blessing in spite of his ambiguous past. He awakens in awe and excitement, naming the place "Beth-El," the gateway to the Divine, proclaiming that "God was here and I did not know it."

Jacob is "everyman" and "everywoman" – we are constantly in the presence of holiness, but are often unaware of it. Only occasionally do we experience the fullness of grace and exclaim in retrospect, "God was here and I did not know it" or, perhaps more boldly, "God was here and now I know." "God is here" is the simple message of Christmas. Every place is a thin place, every act a window into the divine, every encounter a revelation of the angelic. Everyday life is filled with the divine – fixing breakfast, changing a diaper, answering the e-mail or phone, going shopping, meeting with co-workers, driving home with your teenager. God is here and we can know it!

Affirmation: God is here in the everyday moments and encounters of life.

Action: Pray with your eyes open today. Let interruptions as well as scheduled events call you to prayer. See the holiness of those around you. Awaken to your divinity and the wonder of all creation.

Loving and creative God, the whole earth is full of your glory. Let my eyes be open – my senses be full – of your beauty. Let me exclaim throughout the day "You are here, and I am grateful." In Christ's name. Amen.

+++

ELEVENTH DAY OF CHRISTMAS

WHAT DO YOU SAY TO A BURNING BUSH?

Now Moses kept the flock of Jethro his father in law, the priest of Midian: and he led the flock to the backside of the desert, and came to the mountain of God, even to Horeb. And the angel of the LORD *appeared unto him in a flame of fire out of the midst of a bush: and he looked, and, behold, the bush*

> *burned with fire, and the bush was not consumed. And Moses said, I will now turn aside, and see this great sight, why the bush is not burnt. And when the* LORD *saw that he turned aside to see, God called unto him out of the midst of the bush, and said, Moses, Moses. And he said, Here am I. And he said, Draw not nigh hither: put off thy shoes from off thy feet, for the place whereon you stand is holy ground.* (Exodus 3:1-5)

The Jewish tradition is known for a spiritual-intellectual practice known as the *midrash*. Beginning with reflection on the text, a *midrash* seeks the deeper, often metaphorical, spiritual, and theological, meaning of the text. Imaginative and creative, the practice of *midrash* sees the text of scripture as the beginning and not the end of conversation. There is always more light to be shed on scripture, because Divine Wisdom is more that we can encompass or imagine.

In the spirit of *midrash*, the story is told of a group of rabbis who gathered to ponder the question, "Why was the bush burning but not consumed?" The discussion went around and around with many meanings suggested. Finally, one of the rabbis illuminated the conversation when he asserted, "The bush was burning and not consumed, so that one day as Moses passed by he would notice it." God was trying to get Moses' attention with a fiery bush, but

Moses had other things on his mind as he journeyed to work each morning. But, when he paused long enough to behold the marvel, his life was transformed; he encountered God and received his life's vocation.

Could it be that there are bushes all around but we are too busy to notice? Could it be that God is trying to get our attention but we have more pressing matters on our minds? As the Christmas season draws to a close, and it comes and goes so quickly, we ask, "Why can't we keep Christmas all year long?" The answer is: "We can." But, we must be awake to wonder and open to the beauty of the moment. We must pause long enough to let go of our plans to experience the wonder and wisdom God is placing in front of us every moment of the day. This isn't easy for me and may not be for you. Still, we can practice incarnation and live Christmas by a sense of amazement and openness that leads to blessing the world around us. For me, I draw near to Christmas by times of prayer and meditation; going to a quiet place or walking each morning on the beach and then taking the insights and calm I experience to the busyness of daily life. Eyes open, I can, with William Blake, experience eternity in a grain of sand and holiness in the cry of a baby. God is with us, and when we slow down, we can feel the presence of God, moving gently in our lives.

Affirmation: I pause long enough to experience the wonders spread forth along my way.

Action: Throughout the day, take a moment to pause long enough to notice, experience, and respond to the world within and around you. You will discover burning bushes scattered along your daily sojourns.

God of fire and light, help us move from busyness to awareness. Help us pause long enough to see burning bushes everywhere. Let them enlighten us and guide us on our way. In Christ's name. Amen.

+++

THE TWELFTH DAY OF CHRISTMAS

GOD WITH SKIN

And the Word was made flesh, and dwelt among us, (and we beheld his glory, the glory as of the only begotten of the Father,) full of grace and truth. (John 1:14)

Emmanuel means "God with us." God is one of us, experiencing the world through the eyes of Jesus. "The word made flesh" walks among us as God's beloved child, Jesus of Nazareth. God is with us in Bethlehem's manger and God is with us today. We need a God with skin; incarnate and embodied, giving grace and beauty to every moment of life. On the twelfth day of Christmas, let us embrace the spirit of a beloved Christmas carol.

> O holy Child of Bethlehem
> Descend to us, we pray
> Cast out our sin and enter in
> Be born to us today
> We hear the Christmas angels
> The great glad tidings tell
> O come to us, abide with us
> Our Lord Emmanuel.

Affirmation: God is with me in the concrete and embodied events of my life.

Action: In honor of the Bethlehem Christ child, honor the incarnation of "God with skin," in the life of the children of the world. Experience the holiness of children near and far – in your local community as well as overseas. Make a commitment to advocate for children through acts of kindness as well as support of excellent schools, safe neighborhoods, and adequate health care. This isn't political issue of left and right but Christian care for our most vulnerable companions, the children.

Holy and loving Jesus, who blessed the children, help us bless them today. Remind us of the child within in all its innocence. Help us to live gracefully and gratefully caring for every child. In Christ's name. Amen.

+++

THE EPIPHANY OF CHRIST

TAKING ANOTHER PATH HOME

When they had heard the king, they set out; and there, ahead of them, went the star that they had seen at its rising, until it stopped over the place where the child was. When they saw that the star had stopped, they were overwhelmed with joy. On entering the house, they saw the child with Mary his mother; and they knelt down and paid him homage. Then, opening their treasure chests, they offered him gifts of gold, frankincense, and myrrh. And having been warned

> *in a dream not to return to Herod, they left for their own country by another road.* (Matthew 2:9-12)

Sometimes great wisdom can be distilled in a short sentence, barely noticed as the reader focuses on the "main point" of scripture. One of my favorite scriptural passages occurs after the account of the gifts of the magi to the Christ child. Its simplicity captures our own life journeys: "They left for their country by another road."

Life is about alternative pathways, about roads not taken, and paths blocked and ways emerging in the wilderness. Think about how your life has unfolded: Did you ever have to take an alternate pathway after the loss of a job, a divorce, a health crisis, an economic downturn, or unexpected good fortune? Life is never predictable and in the moment, we may have to alter our plans, letting go of one image of the future and opening to another. We often feel disoriented, but moments of disorientation can, as theologian Robert McAfee Brown asserts, awaken us to the surprises of grace. God moves in our lives with a gentle but persistent providence. God doesn't determine the minute or big events of our lives, but is always ready to provide us a number of creative routes to God's far horizon. God is always making a way where we imagined a dead end.

The feast of Epiphany celebrates the coming of the magi. In the Orthodox Christian tradition, it rivals Christmas in its affirmation of God's presence in the baby Jesus. Strangers from another faith tradition, the magi follow a star and give homage to the Child whose love will save us all. They follow a dream, trusting revelation to guide them home and protect an innocent child. Christmas is a holy adventure, an open heart and an imaginative mind. Let us go forth with the words of Howard Thurman, living Christmas each day of the year and that each moment can be an epiphany, a revelation of the living God.

> *When the song of the angels is stilled,*
> *When the star in the sky is gone,*
> *When the kings and the princes are home,*
> *When the shepherds are back with their flock,*
> *The work of Christmas begins:*
> *To find the lost,*
> *To heal the broken,*
> *To feed the hungry,*
> *To release the prisoner,*
> *To rebuild the nations,*

To bring peace among brothers,
To make music in the heart.[5]

Affirmation: Every encounter can be an epiphany, an encounter with the living God.

Action: Look for God's presence in the unexpected and unplanned events of the day. Ask for God's guidance when you need to depart from your prearranged schedule. Let Divine Wisdom show you the path ahead.

God of all peoples, you are present on every pathway. Incline my heart to your wisdom and help me seek your wisdom when old paths lead to dead ends and new paths beckon me. Help me to find joy in the journey. In Christ's name. Amen.

---

[5] Ibid., 28.

GROUP MEETINGS

If your congregation sponsors Advent spirituality groups, these exercises and questions may be helpful to you. As you meet together, remember to give everyone who wishes an opportunity to share their insights. Listen and affirm the many viewpoints in your group, affirming that everyone in the group is being touched by God and can be the source of wisdom.

WEEK ONE
(Advent Days One to Seven)

Begin your group meeting with a time of contemplative prayer. A simple form of contemplation involves closing your eyes and focusing on your breath as a way of connecting with God's Spirit. In the quiet, breathe with attentiveness, open to God's presence and inspiration. If your mind wanders, pause to bring it back to your breath without judgment.

1) What are the greatest challenges you face in living a holy and adventurous Advent? How do you live attentively to God in the midst of the holiday rush and merriment?

2) Do you believe that we will ever experience the peaceable kingdom described by Isaiah?

Do you think we will ever turn swords into plowshares? How can we be part of this peacemaking process?

3) What does the promise of abundant life mean you? What stands in the way of your living abundantly? What keeps others from living abundantly?

4) What do you think about the end of the world prophesies? If we see the world as continuing indefinitely, how might that change our values and priorities? Do we have a role in healing the Earth?

5) What is your prayer style? What do you think of Anne Lamott's threefold prayer, "Help! Thanks! Wow!"? What would it mean for you to "pray without ceasing?"

6) The Apostle Paul asserts that "nothing can separate us from the love of God in Christ Jesus our Lord." What would it mean to you if you actually lived by this scripture?

Conclude your gathering with going around the circle, noting the beauties of life. What beauty are you thankful for? Give thanks for the "wow" moments in life.

WEEK TWO
(Advent Days Eight to Fourteen)

Begin this session by breathing deeply, opening to God's presence. As you breathe, visualize God's Advent light entering your whole being, beginning at the head, then moving to the neck, heart and lungs, stomach and solar plexus, reproductive and digestive systems, and down your legs. Experience God's light surrounding and protecting you. You are in the circle of God's light and love.

1) In what ways does diversity enrich your life? How do spiritual practices open us to greater diversity?

2) Why is the Advent-Christmas season so difficult for persons who are grieving? What do you think of the Apostle Paul's counsel to grieve hopefully?

3) What is the "good news" of Advent? What "good news" do you want to share the world?

4) What is your greatest antidote to the fears of life? What helps you be courageous in difficult times?

5) What actions might you and your church take to live God's kingdom on earth as it is in heaven? How would you have to change your life to be a citizen in God's realm?

6) Have you ever experienced the "call" of God? How would you feel if you heard God call you by name, as Samuel experienced God's presence?

7) Do you think God is present in your life? Do you think God is present in the lives of others?

This week we considered Dag Hammarksjold's statement:

> *For all that has been – thanks!*
> *For all that shall be – yes!*

As you conclude this time, for what things are you most thankful? What big "yeses" lie ahead for you?

WEEK THREE
(Advent Days Fifteen to Twenty-one)

Take time as a group to read prayerfully the following scripture from Day Twenty Two: Now the birth of Jesus the Messiah took place in this way. When his mother Mary had been engaged to Joseph, but before they lived together, she was found to be with child from the Holy Spirit. Her husband Joseph, being a righteous man and unwilling to expose her to public disgrace, planned to dismiss her quietly. But just when he had resolved to do this, an angel of the Lord appeared to him in a dream and said, "Joseph, son of David, do not be afraid to take Mary as your wife, for the child conceived in her is from the Holy Spirit. She will bear a son, and you are to name him Jesus, for he will save his people from their sins." (Matthew 1:18-21)

Put yourself in Joseph's place. How might you respond to Mary's unexpected pregnancy? How might you respond to dreaming about an angelic visitor? What role do dreams have in your spiritual life?

1) Read Mary's Magnificat (Luke 1:46-55). What do you make of Mary's words? How might her words motivate action in our current economic and national life?

2) A popular saying proclaims, "Prayer changes things." What is your experience with praying for persons and events? Do you think your prayers make a difference? Can we pray for a healing, a sense of nearness of God, even when there cannot be a cure?

3) What do you think of Madeleine L'Engle's statement, "I believe in God with all my doubts"? In what ways can doubt be beneficial to faith? What are the doubts that complement your beliefs?

4) Even though God may not be the source of life's dark moments, can we learn something and

deepen our faith in times of disorientation and darkness?

5) How would your life change if you made a commitment to "see Christ in everyone?"

6) Our calling is to see our blessings as an opportunity to bless others. What are your greatest perceived blessings? In what ways do these inspire you to reach out to others? How might you bless others?

Take a few minutes to look back on the past three weeks. What has been your greatest learning? When have you felt closest to God in the course of this study? What have been your greatest challenges?

THE CHRISTMAS SEASON

The weeks between Christmas and Epiphany may prove difficult for gathering a group together. However, if your group meets, you may find these group practices inspirational and spiritually helpful.

WEEK ONE
(Christmas Days One to Eight)

Please meditate as a group on the following passage: So the shepherds went with haste and found Mary and Joseph, and the child lying in the manger. When they saw this, they made known what had been told them about this child; and all who heard it were amazed at what the shepherds told them. But Mary treasured all these words and pondered them in her heart. (Luke 2:17-19) *Put yourself in the position of the shepherds. How would you feel? Seeing yourself as Mary, how would you feel? What does it mean to treasure memories in your heart?*

1) Take time to reflect on your Christmas experiences. What was your most memorable Christmas? What was special about that Christmas?

2) What does it mean to be created in God's image? More personally, what does it mean for *you* to be created in God's image?

3) Ponder Herod's murder of the children in Nazareth. (Day Four of Christmas) Where are children at risk in your community? Where are children at risk in the world? If every child is a hidden Christ-child, how might you best protect and affirm the children? What tangible action can you and your church take?

4) In light the grandeur of the universe, reflect as a group on the words of Psalm 8:

When I look at your heavens, the work of your fingers, the moon and the stars that you have established; what are human beings that you are mindful of them, mortals that you care for them? Yet you have made them a little lower than God, and *crowned them with glory and honor.*

What does it mean for you to be a little lower than God? How do you feel about our place in the immensity of the universe? Take time as a group to look up the words of "How Great Thou Art." How do they shape your understanding of God and the universe?

Conclude by pondering the statement from the Psalm 19:1. Where are you experiencing God's glory? Give thanks for the beauty of God's world.

WEEK TWO
(Christmas Day Eight to Feast of the Epiphany)

After a time of quiet contemplation, opening to God's enlightening presence, meditate on the following words: Let this mind be in you, which was also in Christ Jesus: Who, being in the form of God, thought it not robbery to be equal with God: But made himself of no reputation, and took upon him the form of a servant, and was made in the likeness of men: And being found in fashion as a man, he humbled himself, and became obedient unto death, even the death of the cross. Wherefore God also hath highly exalted him, and given him a name which is above every name: That at the name of Jesus every knee should bow, of things in heaven, and things in earth, and things under the earth; And that every tongue should confess that Jesus Christ is Lord, to the glory of God the Father. (Philippians 2:5-11) *What do these words say about Christ's relationship to you and the world? How do these words nurture your own spiritual experience?*

1) Philippians 2:5-11 describes two kinds of power, unilateral and coercive power and relational and affirming power. How does Christ's power transform our understandings and practices of power?

2) John counsels us to "have the mind of Christ." What would it mean to have the mind of Christ? What would it be like to experience the world as Christ does?

3) If God came to you with the question, "What do you want me to do for you?" how would you respond? What are the greatest gifts God can give you?

4) Where have you experienced "thin places" that reveal God's presence? Have you ever experienced a "ladder of angels" revealing God to you in everyday life? What is it like to pray with your eyes open?

5) Have you ever gone by another road than you anticipated? What events changed your life? How did you adapt to new possibilities? Was God present in the unexpected detours and pathways?

Conclude with a reading of Howard Thurman's poem, "The Work of Christmas." Ask for God to open you to the gift of Christmas. Pray that Christ be born in you and the world.

www.ingramcontent.com/pod-product-compliance
Lightning Source LLC
Chambersburg PA
CBHW061447040426
42450CB00007B/1253